HOLLAND'S HOUSE

HOLLAND'S HOUSE

A NATION BUILDING A HOME

*

A SHORT STORY TOLD

BY

PETER BRICKLAYER

*

WITH PICTURES

BY

JO SPIER

*

PRINTED BY

JOH. ENSCHEDÉ EN ZONEN, HAARLEM, HOLLAND

1939

HOLLAND'S PLACE
UNDER THE SUN

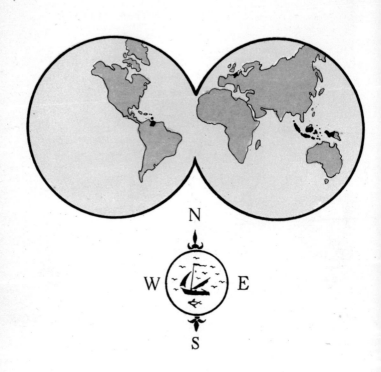

CONTENTS

THE GATE
OF HOLLAND

I. THE WALLS GO UP

Tomorrow's world! . . .

Man is restlessly preparing for it, and always has been, and always will be. For he who is content with yesterday, gets behind the times.

And what man does, nations do. For nations are men and soil and adventure put together. The never ending task of building tomorrow's world by human effort began with our pre-historic ancestors and will go on as long as this good earth lasts.

This little book wants to tell the short story of a small nation building a large home. It's true, our story could be long enough, for endless energy, daring, success and disillusion, endless thought, faith, enterprise, struggle, defeat and victory were sunk into the long centuries of Dutch history, ever since a handful of huntsmen camped, some 2000 years B.C., in the higher parts of what is present day Holland. High and dry, safe from the surrounding waters, treacherous rivers and an unruly sea. That, in a sense, still is Holland's problem. Only, and since there was not enough high, they had, after growing more numerous, to be content with low, and to surround themselves with dikes to supplement nature's own encourage-ment: an occasional row of dunes, to keep the water out. They still do that today, in 1939, wrestling their twelfth province away from underneath the tamed waves of the Zuyder Zee.

About old man Hollander of those dark ages of 2000 B.C. very little is known. Even his tomorrow vanishes into a thick fog. History refused to become much clearer until the restless

Romans, about fifty years before the beginning of our Christian era, visited these sodden parts of North Western Europe, where three large rivers, Rhine, Meuse and Scheldt, flow into the North Sea, and where, for a while, the unpolished local tribes were turned into outposts of Roman imperial splendour.

Caveman-stuff, these Batavians, Kaninefates, Frisians and others, and, according to our standards of today, not extremely civilized people. But already imbued with that love of liberty and self-government which was destined to remain the prevailing characteristic of the nation into which they were going to be moulded and developed during the centuries to come.

They revolted against their foreign masters, they fought amongst themselves. They mixed with new tribes, Franks and Saxons. Gradually the 'low countries' became a full house. There were freemen and bondmen, the former owning the land, and the latter, the serfs, working it for them. Primitive society, but containing already the seeds from which a more complicated social and political structure of nobles and commoners, rulers and ruled would germinate before long.

The Roman empire crumpled up towards the end of the fourth century, and left the low countries to themselves. Christian missionaries slowly conquered the field, and prepared the ground in which Dutch theological ardour was going to strike root very deeply and permanently. Charlemagne's powerful hand reached out and brought law and order. His feudal lords ruled the low lands in his name, collected taxes, administered justice and sometimes injustice. Out of a system of decentralized power rose feudalism, creating a conglomeration of smaller units, estates, townships, jealous of each others means and might. And after Charlemagne's empire broke up, the low lands, early in the 10th century, found themselves belonging as a duchy to Germany.

Again the local lords, ruling the country in the name of the emperor, became the real strongholds of power. It was from them, not from the absentee central government, that the people craved and obtained protection against the ruthless Norsemen who swept these regions between the years 800 and 1000. Their influence increased as their territory grew by inheritance, purchase or conquest. And so, slowly but surely, a new political design began to show its contours. Around the personalities of successive and successful feudal lords and tenants crystallized political and administrative units: counties and duchies like Flanders, Holland and Gelderland, owing allegiance to the German emperor, but often refusing to be over-ruled, as their own power and authority steadily augmented. A struggle, one might say, for state rights against federal authority, so well known in American history, but adapted and translated into terms of 12th century Europe. Still, a thing to be remembered when, three or four hundred years later, the world witnesses the birth of the Dutch nation.

The counts of Holland (the 12th century county, not the complete Netherlands of a later period), ambitiously sought to extend their possessions. So did others, and amongst these neighbours there was little quiet and peace. A costly war game was at the order of the day, requiring lots of men, material and money. Gradually the towns and their most prosperous burghers saw their chance and demonstrated a remarkable talent to seize it. In return for financial and other assistance they obtained all

HOLLAND TOO HAS ITS
SKYSCRAPERS!

BUT NOT SO MUCH BECAUSE
HOLLAND'S HOUSES ARE
HIGH, AS BECAUSE HOLLAND'S
SKIES ARE SO LOW. ~

Iospius.

kinds of rights and privileges, in other words: freedom to live their own lives to a certain extent, an early form of what we call autonomy today. Pretty soon no ruler could hope to succeed without the help of his important townships. The free burgher became a considerable power in the feudal state. His wits and money began to hold their own against the steel armour of the mediaeval 'upper classes'.

We must hurry, because this is supposed to be a short story. And so we run along and mention in very few words the influence of the crusades, when those who took part in them, were rewarded with new freedom to establish themselves as tradesmen and artisans in the cities. Whereas, on the other hand, the devoted and adventurous knights who equipped their expeditionary forces for the Holy Land, were obliged to borrow more money from the towns, which developed rapidly into centres of trade and industry, and obtained more and more power and privileges in exchange for their indispensable financial collaboration.

We must also skip many names and events. In a nutshell: The county of Holland and Zeeland passed into the hands of Hainault. In turn Hainault went over to the House of Bavaria, towards the middle of the 14th century. Flanders was annexed by the duchy of Burgundy, together with Brabant and Limburg. Then, in 1433, the Bavarian dominion in the north became united with the Burgundian estates in the south. A new move towards centralized government became apparent. But against this Holland and Zeeland raised objections, and they succeeded in securing special sovereign privileges in several respects. For a moment the marriage between Mary of Burgundy and Maximilian, son of the German emperor, again seemed to reinforce the centralist tendencies, but Burgundy itself was lost to France, and in Flanders, Holland, Gelderland and Friesland strong movements in favor of regional autonomy were dominating the situation.

This was the state of affairs which Mary's son, Philip of Burgundy, found when he entered into power. By marriage he gained the throne of Spain. His son, Charles V, thus inherited the vast realm of which the 'low countries', for many reasons, had become a rather uneasy possession, unable to forget their longing for self government and freedom. But Charles had not forgotten the difficulties which his father and grandmother had experienced with those free-minded burghers and their proud and wealthy nobles. At once he threw his great weight into the scales to further the cause of more centralization of government and administration. By 1543 he had succeeded in uniting all the Netherlands provinces into one dominion, at the head of which he placed his sister Mary. The provincial representatives, nobles and others, were allowed to assist her in an advisory capacity. The Netherlands consisted now of seventeen provinces with more than 200 walled cities and many other towns and villages, a prosperous and highly civilized European corner, where commerce, shipping, fisheries, cattle-rearing, weaving industries, architecture and the fine arts had learned to thrive notwithstanding continuous wars and political upheavals. But as yet there existed no consciousness of a common fate, no feeling of super-provincial solidarity, of national unity. To be sure, there were common interests in the economic field, there were cultural bonds, there was, in the northern provinces, a freedom of mind which made them perhaps more accessible to the spirit of a new era: Erasmus, Columbus, Luther, Copernicus, Calvin: philosophy, reformation, science, discovery. The birth of the Dutch nation however could only result from a supreme effort to defend life and liberty of body and soul against a common tyrannical enemy.

The clash was bound to come. Philip II, son of Charles V, was a religious fanatic, who set himself the task to fight the Reformation to the very last heretic. The absolute power which, in Spain, he had inherited from his father, was the surest means to antagonize the Dutch, who had learned to consider the liberties, conquered during long centuries of struggle and self-education, as cherished possessions which they, in the age of humanism, would not willingly surrender. Charles V had tried to enforce his will with tactful respect for existing public feeling. Philip, totally unable to see the Dutch point of view, or, for that matter, any other point of view but his own, chose to disregard the very things most dear to those who had, from their very debut on this scene, been endeavouring to establish and safeguard certain elementary rights of self-determination.

Margaret of Parma, Philip's half sister, was appointed regent, and a cardinal, Granvelle, who of course could hardly be expected to show a lenient attitude towards the gaining Reformation in the Netherlands, became her chief advisor. The cruel persecutions of the Dutch protestants by the Spanish Inquisition went even so far as to antagonize many faithful members of the Roman Catholic Church. At the same time a movement sprang up to regain more regional political freedom. Feeling running very high, the storm broke when, in 1568, an exited mob in Antwerp raided catholic churches. General confusion ensued. Some of the nobles, judging that this violent opposition took a dangerous turn fled back to the side of the Spanish king. But William of Orange, then stadtholder of Holland and Zeeland (governor, in a sense, of these two Dutch provinces under Philips' supreme authority), refused to follow their example. A great name, of one who was destined to become the father of a free and united nation, appeared. And history, without being aware of it, entered upon a new chapter.

In 1567, Philip's emissary, the Duke of Alva, had arrived in the Netherlands to fight heresy without pardon and collect taxes for the depleted Spanish exchequer from most un-Spanish subjects, subdued by force. He was a loyal servant of his King, no doubt, but hardly the man to win Dutch hearts. Before a special court, soon known as the 'bloody tribunal', he dragged all those who dared to contest Philip's claim to put the souls of free men in chains, torment their bodies and trample upon their human rights. By publicly executing some of the leading members of the Dutch nobility Alva sought to intimidate the dissenters. But soon he had to face a hostile army, which William of Orange, after temporarily taking refuge in Germany, had organized to deliver the Netherlands from the Spanish fury.

And so, in 1568 , the great war started, a struggle for religious and political freedom and selfdetermination; a war which was to last eighty long years, but under whose awful weight and misery, the Dutch nation was welded together in the scorching flames.

THE DEATH OF THE FOUNDING FATHER:
THE END OF A MAN, THE BEGINNING OF
AN IDEA ~

A new day dawned. A leader stood up and offered his life to an ideal: a nation of free and tolerant men, finding each other in united opposition against foreign tyranny. The story of William the Silent has been told many times. It is a story of perseverance, against adversities, and sometimes against the misunderstandings of those he tried to save; the story of an unselfish man, leading the headstrong components of an unformed nation, often divided against itself, towards independence and responsibility. The story also of a heroic effort, ultimately crowned with the fulfilment of its essential aims. The story, finally, of the foundation of that uneradicable relationship between the House of Orange and the people of the Netherlands, which, after 350 years still expresses itself in the love and unshakable loyalty wherewith the Dutch nation surrounds the royal descendents of the founding father, William the Silent, William of Orange, Father William.

Builder of a nation's tomorrow.

II. THE ROOF IS PUT ON

Freedom, unwisely administered, can become a source of weakness. William of Orange, seeking strength in unity, strove hard to keep his lowlanders together. At first he almost succeeded, but soon the southern provinces where catholicism prevailed and the calvinistic north drifted apart, and the Spanish adversaries naturally made the most of it. In the catholic south the defenders of the Holy Church were in a favorable position to create confusion and wavering. There were cases of desertion and king Philip gained a point or two. The north, in reaction, pulled itself together. Under the exertion of John of Nassau, William's brother, the seven northern provinces in 1579 concluded a political compact, known as the Union of Utrecht. It meant a separation between north and south, between what would henceforth be called the Spanish Netherlands and the United Provinces of the North. But these United Provinces became the foundation on which the Republic of the United Netherlands was to be raised, as an independent, sovereign nation.

King Philip retorted by setting a price on the head of William the Silent, and by proclaiming him a traitor. It proved to be the last straw that made the scales turn. On the 26th of July 1581 the States General of the United Provinces went into conference at The Hague and solemnly declared that Philip had forfeited his sovereignty over them, and that they held themselves absolved from any allegiance to him, whatsoever. From that day on they considered themselves free to decide their own fate.

Americans, who read this brief account, will recognize some

THE BIRTH OF A NATION

of their own experiences. There is indeed a curious historical parallel. The 26th of July 1581 is to Holland what the 4th of July 1776 is to the United States. In their Act of Abjuration the States General wrote words which were going to find an echo, a little less than twohundred years later, in Philadelphia.

'A prince—they stated—is appointed by God to be the shepherd of His people. When he fails in this duty, when he oppresses them, violates their rights, and tramples on their liberties, as if they were slaves, then he is not a prince but a tyrant. And the Estates of the land are then justified in deposing him and placing another on his throne'.

Compare to this the American Declaration of Independence of the Continental Congress, abjuring King George III, in which it is said:

'We hold these truths to be self evident, that all men are created equal, that they are endowed by their creator with certain unalienable rights, that among these are life, liberty and the pursuit of happiness. That to secure these rights governments are instituted among men, deriving their just powers from the consent of the governed. That whenever any form of government becomes destructive of these ends, it is the right of the people to alter or to abolish it . . . The history of the present King of Great Britain is a history of repeated injuries and usurpations, all having in direct object the establishment of an absolute tyranny over these States . . . We therefore, the representatives of the United States of America . . . solemnly publish and declare that these colonies are, and of right ought to be, free and independent states, that they are absolved from all allegiance to the British crown . . '

The United Provinces of the Netherlands impeaching a Spanish king, the United States of America impeaching an English king! History repeats itself, but it does more than that. It carries a great thought, a great faith, a great principle, far into the ages. The love of freedom, the feeling for tolerance and mutual respect, the refusal to be governed without an equitable share in the controlling power and a reasonable influence on public affairs, such were the spiritual and political forces which decided the fate of Hollanders and Americans alike. Two nations born in struggle to free their souls. Two nations where the flame of freedom and tolerance is still burning . . .

But we must return to the Dutch revolution, to those not too well organized partners in revolt, who were now facing one of the longest and bitterest wars history has ever known. Help was sorely needed. And no three thousand miles of protecting ocean separated these game fighters from their powerful former master!

French support was sought, and when it ultimately failed, an appeal was made to England's Queen Elizabeth. But a year before, Philip had finally triumphed over Orange. His body, not his soul. A murderer, believing to serve his God and his most catholic King, penetrated into William's house at Delft, and fired the fatal shot. But around the dead body of their leader the Dutch now closed their ranks more firmly than ever before. A man was killed, a source of endless inspiration had been set flowing.

The war raged on. And the military genius of William's sons, Maurice and Frederick Henry, served to strengthen the position of the United Provinces enormously. Europe began to sit up and take notice of the new state, and in 1596 a triple alliance was concluded between the Dutch, England and France. It was the formal recognition of the United Provinces as a sovereign power. Thirteen years later a rather exhausted Spain agreed to a truce, concluding the treaty with the Dutch 'in the quality of free states'. But at the expiration of this interval, in 1621, the war broke out once more. Again—but with mixed feelings—French assistance was obtained, and a strong Dutch navy won a number of crushing victories over the Spaniards, who had been weakened by the revolt of Portugal and the loss of the Portuguese colonies in the East and West Indies. Peace came in sight and an eighty years battle for a free national existence drew towards a close. On the 30th of January 1648 the peace treaty was signed at Munster. The United Provinces were recognized as a free and independent state, the former Spanish trade monopoly in the East and West Indies was abolished, and all the conquests won by the Dutch from the Portuguese [formerly under Spanish rule] were ceded to the Dutch republic. The United Netherlands were now firmly established, powerful and respected. A nation had built a house with many rooms. And the roof had now been put on.

But the young house would have to weather many storms, which rattled its doors and windows, and sometimes threatened to tear off the roof altogether, and blow the whole thing to pieces. There were internal disputes, the Orange federalists and the state-rights-parties came to loggerheads, as federalists and state righters are wont to do in our own twentieth century in other Unions. Again the old conflict between centralized and

25

decentralized power, so interwoven with Dutch history from the time of the Roman legions along the Rhine, raised its many dragonheads. On the high sea a struggle for supremacy with England was brewing, and it would take three wars to decide the matter in favor of the British. Ambitious designs of the French 'Sun King', Louis XIV, had to be checked, and it took all the genius of another member of the House of Orange, William III, great grandson of the Silent, to save the Netherlands from being permanently defeated by French armies, those very lowlands where the Spanish legions once had contested their claim to a national life.

With the death in 1702 of William III, that remarkable statesman, who since 1689 also occupied the throne of England, and who lies buried in Westminster Abbey, as the one and only Dutch prince who ruled over Holland, England and England's American colonies—a Dutch King with American subjects in other words—the line of direct descendents of William the Silent came to an abrupt end. Again a great leader was torn away in a most difficult period of national development. The United Provinces seemed at times to be not quite so united as circumstances demanded. The result was a gradual dwindling of power, and a declining influence upon European politics. But on becoming involved in new wars —and there always was an entangling war somewhere in Europe in those days—the people turned, as of old, towards a prince of the ever faithful House of Orange: now William IV, of the Frisian line, again prepared to serve the nation for which his illustrious ancestor had laid down his life.

Our story has now reached the 18th century. The centre of

HOLLAND'S FAITHFUL ALLY IN
TIMES OF WAR: THE WATER.

European power shifted and moved further and further away from the Netherlands. The American revolution found the Provinces under the leadership of stadtholder William V, and with a strong sympathy in the hearts of the people for the revolting colonies in the New World, who fought a battle which in so many respects recalled to the Dutch their own struggle for liberty. These feelings coupled with marked indignation caused by British action against neutral shipping on the high seas, pushed the Netherlands into another war with England, resulting this time in the loss of certain East Indian possessions, and fresh internal trouble between the Orangists and their opponents, the so called 'patriot party'.

History moves quickly now. The French revolution, for all its ideological altruism, meant another French effort to obtain a firm foothold in the low countries, important strategical corner in North Western Europe. The 'patriot party', taking sides with the new revolutionary philosophy, and carelessly admitting its foreign policy as well, went so far as to welcome with great rejoicings the French armies invading the Provinces. The stadtholder and his family, unable to stem the tide, fled to England. The house of the Dutch nation, so proudly conceived by those who sacrificed their blood to free themselves from foreign domination, shook in its foundations. It even changed its name to 'Batavian Republic', and became closely allied with the French. But French alliance meant French domination, and entanglements in the wars of the Revolution. What price glory? The Dutch colonies were lost to England, commerce was ruined. Meanwhile in France Napoleonic dictatorship had succeeded revolutionary freedom, whatever that had turned out to be in practice. And the Emperor, with a keen eye for strategic and economic values, reorganized the Netherlands into a kingdom, and forced his brother Louis to become the unwilling king of an unwilling people. Four years later, in 1810, Louis abdicated and Napoleon incorporated Holland, as the whole national unit was now named, into the French empire.

The house stood silent now, with lowered curtains. A monument of forgotten fame in a darkening cemetery . . .

Once again the Dutch had to bow to a foreign ruler. Once again it chafed their hearts and stabbed their pride. Once again it brought them together and stirred their longings for that freedom their ancestors had conquered at so costly a price from a Spanish tyrant. Only to lose it, one hundred and sixty years later, to a Corsican one?

But Napoleon's star dipped at Leipzig in 1813, and at once the revolt which had been fermenting in the Netherlands, broke into the light. The son of the last stadtholder was recalled from England, and again a member of the House of Orange took the helm, this time not as a stadtholder but as a sovereign prince of a nation which had recovered a vigorous and irrepressible will to live. The Congress of Vienna, reorganizing Europe after the final decision of Waterloo, confirmed the new order. The southern territories of the old Spanish Netherlands, which today form Belgium, were joined with the northern United Provinces into the new Kingdom of the Netherlands, with the son and heir of stadtholder William V on the royal throne as *King* William I. A powerful state, situated between mighty neighbours, and holding a strategical position which none of the others was likely to trust between the hands of someone else.

Holland's house, free again and strong, shone with new splendour. But the union between north and south, which, centuries earlier, had only been possible under foreign predominance, and had even failed to hold good against the common Spanish enemy during the eighty years war, would not last. Like America, greater Holland knew its civil war, and in 1830 the southern provinces bolted. Intervention of the great powers forced Holland to acquiesce in a definite separation. The State of Belgium, under a monarch of its own, was founded, and henceforth the Kingdom of the Netherlands, direct descendant of the old United Northern Provinces, started on a national course, which has remained unaltered unto this very day.

At the wheel the Orange dynasty is still on watch. Three kings, each bearing the historic name of the founding father, William, have reigned and died. The present queen, Wilhelmina, again dedicating her name to that devoted Silent, has recently celebrated the fortieth anniversary of her accession to the throne amidst the unanimous rejoicings of a grateful people. And at her side, her daughter, crown princess Juliana, whose name—again— is a tribute to William the Silent's wise and noble mother, prepares herself for the high office which, in years to come, will claim her responsibility. Her husband prince Bernhardt, has easily conquered the hearts of the people by his cheerful personality. And with their little daughter, the princess Beatrix, the old dynastic Orange tree is blossoming out with fresh vitality into new bloom.

Today the house of Holland stands confident and resilient under its sturdy roof, with the old colours flying, as they did

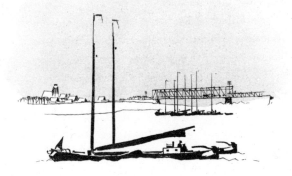

SOMEWHERE
IN HOLLAND.

J. Spur

in the days of William the Father; the orange, and the red, white, blue.

The sky above is sometimes cloudy.

But the old banners stream out, into the new day . . .

III. NEW ROOMS

The walls were hardly up, when the Dutch began to feel that their house was too small for their number, their maintenance, their energies. And that was not so surprising. The fact that most of their country was situated from two to sixteen feet below sea-level had made them very much aware of the presence of the water. When they were not building dikes to prevent the north western storms from flooding the land with the North Sea, they were building other dams to prevent the great rivers from doing exactly the same with the melted snow from the mountains of central and south western Europe. But having walled themselves in sufficiently well to be able to look the ocean in the face, not as an enemy but as a somewhat un-ruly friend, they learned to appreciate its more profitable qualities, and turned fishermen and seafarers.

The man who lives behind a dike, is like a mountaineer: he wants to climb on top to scout for a wider horizon. And if the other side is water, he feels inclined to go and explore it, es-pecially if his little bit of soil offers only limited possibilities for self sufficiency.

So the Dutch took to the water, down to the sea in ships, and ventured out, far away, under strange stars. They had heard about Marco Polo, the Venetian, who, late in the 13th century, had traveled the overland route to China and India. They had been told the story of the Portuguese navigators who, in 1486, rounded Cape Good Hope by force of storm and mistake, thus preparing the way for Vasco de Gama's discovery in 1498 of the complete south eastern sea route to the East Indies, six

BUILDING ITS EMPIRE, HOLLAND LOST MANY SHIPS ....

BUILDING ITS EMPIRE, HOLLAND
LOST PIONEERING AIRPLANES ....

BUILDING ITS EMPIRE, HOLLAND
LOST DARING MEN ....

BUT HOLLAND DID NOT LOOSE ITS
COURAGE, AND GAINED ITS RIGHTFUL
PLACE ON THE HIGHWAYS OF THE WORLD.

years after Columbus, trying out the western direction, had discovered America, when he expected to find India, and accordingly named the dark skinned natives Indians, Red Indians to be exact. They knew that Magellan in 1520 had found the south western sea route to the Philippines by sailing along the east coast of Brazil and the Argentine, until he found the narrow strait, now bearing his name, through which he finally reached the Pacific Ocean. They had found to their regret that the Spaniards and the Portuguese had more or less divided what seemed to be in those days the outer world: the east for the Portuguese, the west for Spain. The best they could do was, for the time being, to send their ships with northern wheat from the Baltic to Cadiz and Lisbon, and become the chief carriers of the eastern produce unloaded there, for distribution in northern Europe.

Just then their eighty years war against the Spaniards started, and it became necessary as well as profitable to beat the enemy at his own commercial game. And after the union between Spain and Portugal in 1581, the Spaniards naturally tried to keep the Dutch enemy away from the Lisbon trade, and in so doing, forced these 'beggars' as they decried them, to sail their ships the whole way to the far east. In those days, however, it was still possible to keep a sea route secret, and the key to the secret remained in Spanish and Portuguese hands.

But the Dutch character is always at its best when all things go wrong. There was a war on, and a very desperate one at that. They were hardly sufficiently organized to present a united front to the armies of king Philip. Yet their merchants and shipowners found time and money to go out experimenting all the same. They sent out hardy skippers like Heemskerk and Barendtsz to discover a route eastward by the north of Siberia so as to be free from interference from Spaniards and Portuguese. And when these efforts remained unsuccessful, they decided to fight the enemy on his own ground, or rather on water he claimed to be his own, and to penetrate into the Indies by way of Cape Good Hope and the Indian Ocean. On the 2nd of April 1595 their first expedition sailed from Holland, Cornelis Houtman commanding. They found the trail and reached their aim. For the Hollanders the call of the east now rang out with a loud voice. Several trading companies were formed, fighting their own battles, reaping their own profits, risking their own losses. Until the States General of the United Provinces of the Northern Netherlands in 1602 combined them all into one chartered Dutch East India Company, with extensive powers to regulate the eastern trade which became their monopoly, discharge the functions of a government in those remote and unsafe East Indian islands and waters, and, not to be forgotten amongst these pioneering adventures, carry on the war with Spain and Portugal. For that the Company was authorized to maintain armed forces, to make war and peace with the native potentates, and to exercise full administrative, judicial and legislative authority over the whole sphere of its operations.

It was the beginning of a union between the Netherlands and the Dutch East Indies, which would slowly and gradually develop from a relationship between exploiters and exploited into one between cooperating parts of a peaceful commonwealth. We shall hear more of it presently.

The south eastern route had been found. Still, there was always the chance of loosing a good cargo to the enemy, who had every reason to keep the rebellious United Provinces from strengthening their financial reserves by a profitable far eastern trade. Hope was still cherished to be able to blaze a trail through the icy polar regions of the north. The Dutch East India Company, shortly before the 12 years truce between Spain and the Netherlands was signed in April 1609, acquired the services of an English captain, Henry Hudson, who on two previous occasions, had been up north to find the coveted passage through the Arctic Ocean. He took the job for 800 Dutch florins, and a promise of 200 more for his wife in case he would fail to come back alive. A small vessel, the 'Half Moon', was placed at his disposal, with definite instructions to steer north and north east. Three days before the truce with Spain was agreed upon, Hudson sailed. It was the 6th of April 1609. But having gone as far as Nova Zembla, he apparently did not like the look of the icebergs and things, turned his ship, and resolutely set out for the eastern shores of America, hoping to find a north American equivalent of the strait to the Pacific, such as Magellan, nearly a century earlier, had discovered in the south. What this English skipper on a Dutch ship actually did find, was the river Hudson. On the 2nd of September 1609 the 'Half Moon's look-out sighted Sandy Hook; on September 4th they passed what is now Coney Island, and established their first and not quite friendly contact with the feathered New Yorkers of those days, valiant Redskins and entirely within their rights. On September 15th Henry Hudson moved as far as present day Albany, and on October 4th anchors were heaved for the return voyage. New Netherland has been discovered by a Dutch ship. And by mistake!

But the directors of the East India Company wanted their skipper to bring home the bacon, and not a mere travelogue. Consequently their enthousiasm was none too great. An occasional ship visited the new shores and left a few irregular campers. There was some fur trade, but the far east absorbed too much energy and too many profitable investments to leave much eagerness for new engagements in the west. Still, there were possibilities. Other countries had sent colonists and settlers to the north American coasts. And there were always the Spaniards and Portuguese in South and Central America to be considered and fought. For the twelve years truce was nearing its end.

For all these reasons in the same year 1621 in which war with Spain was resumed, the Dutch West India Company came into being. America's east and Africa's west coasts were its exploration fields and one of the purposes — in keeping with the ethical standards of the times — was to secure cheap supplies of negro slaves from Africa for the territorial possessions it hoped to acquire in the new world.

Early in 1624 a serious effort to establish a regular settlement along the Hudson river was undertaken by the new Company. The good ship 'New Netherland', carrying thirty families, mostly Walloons from the southern provinces, but under contract to the Company, crossed the Ocean and sailed as far as today's Albany, where Fort Orange was constructed for the protection of the colonists. A second ship followed in April 1625, with an engineer of the Company on board, Crijn

41

Fredericksz, who had orders to erect another fortification further south. The most southern point of Manhattan Island, where The Battery is today, was chosen. And by building Fort Nieuw Amsterdam on the very spot whence the strong nerve racking economic life of the biggest metropolis of all times, New York, now broadcasts its throbbing heart beats to every corner of the world, the Dutch, their hands full with a violent war for the freedom of their own national life, laid, in this new world, the foundations for the greatest city of another republic, that was to follow the Dutch example one hundred and fifty years later: the United States of America.

The house that Holland built was now a structure of considerable dimensions. In the east it had strongholds not only in Batavia, but also at other points of the Malay Archipelago, as well as in Malacca, Ceylon, Cape Good Hope, in Siam and in the Persian Gulf. Dutch sailors also discovered and explored towards the middle of the 17th century the northern shores of Australia and the outskirts of New Zealand, without however actually occupying any of these territories. In the West New Netherland was settled. Further south, and east of Porto Rico, the isles of Saba, St. Martin and St. Eustatius were occupied between the years 1634 and 1648, and still further south, the isles of Curaçao, Bonaire and Aruba. But greater conquests were achieved on the mainland of South America. At the expense of Spain and Portugal a firm footing was obtained in Pernambuco, and the governor, count John Maurice of Nassau who, in 1636, came over from Holland (where his town house at The Hague is now one of the principal musea

THE
HALF MOON"

of old paintings) energetically asserted Dutch supremacy all along the Brazilian coast. Had he been allowed by his Dutch board of directors to invest his commercial profits into the great scheme he had in mind for the development of these colonies, he might have founded under the red, white and blue, an equivalent of what the Dutch East Indies are today. But his employers wanted their profits for home consumption, and so a great opportunity was lost.

Everywhere in the world the Dutch flag was now flying: in Europe, where the United Provinces were victoriously concluding their war against Spain; in Africa, where their trading post, established in 1652 at Cape Good Hope, would in later years become the nucleus of the free Boer Republics which finally amalgamated into the Union of South Africa; in Asia, where the Dutch East India Company was supreme in the Malaysian islands; in Australia and New Zealand where they made their discoveries; and last but by no means least, in the Americas, South, Central and North.

With good reason the Dutch call the 17th century their 'golden age'. A rather amazing age too! Here was a small nation, in the middle of a long and severe battle for its independence, setting out to fight its enemies in all the seven seas, and using its wits quite as deftly as its strength, by reaching out for carefully chosen far distant treasuries which, wisely exploited, would provide them with the means to carry on their war and make a handsome profit besides.

Holland's house had grown very large. In fact, it had become too large. It was no longer possible for the family to keep an eye on every room, and to see to it that, at night, all doors

44

were safely locked. They were not quite sure, where to concentrate their attention, and how to distribute their best talent, their most enterprising capital and their means of power. They had a very wide front to defend, and quite a number of enemies to deal with, at home and abroad. And so, by and by they lost ground again in some of their outlying possessions. The territory in Brazil was finally abandoned to a liberated Portugal in 1662. The English, once awakened to the significance of sea power, having become formidable naval and commercial rivals on the ocean, raided and seized in 1664, between two official wars with Holland, New Netherland, and henceforth Nieuw Amsterdam lives on as New York. A world-famous Dutch admiral, De Ruyter, did his utmost to take the British to account for this act of robbery. He even sailed his ships up their own Medway as far as Chatham, burned the English fleet as it lay at anchor, and created a panic in London. When finally, in July 1667, peace was signed, the terms were, on the whole, not unfavourable to the Dutch. But New Netherland and New Amsterdam were and remained lost. In exchange Holland obtained a piece of land on the north eastern coast of South America, where it looked as though some of the tropical merchandise could be successfully raised, such as, in the far east, had offered many highly profitable opportunities. In this way New Netherland was swapped for Dutch Guyana, or Suriname as it is called now. Not a very clever deal, from the Dutch point of view, considering what lofty heights the old New Amsterdam has reached under the impetus of the star spangled banner . . .

The last Dutch governor of New Netherland, Peter Stuyve-

DID THE BURGHER OF NEW NETHER-
LAND WHO PUT UP THE SIGN AT
THE CORNER OF 17TH CENTURY
WALL-STREET AND BROADWAY REALISE
THAT HE WAS CHRISTENING THE HEART
OF THE WORLD ?

Spie

sant, after surrendering New Amsterdam to the British for lack of adequate support, took his leave and retired with his famous, silver-banded wooden leg to his farm in the Bowery where he died. He had been up against great difficulties, and his authority had not been uncontested. But he left behind a political system based on free municipal government, with the aid of freely chosen representatives of the people. A system which had come to stay, and which, in its essentials, still prevails in the cities of the full grown United States of 1939 as a permanent souvenir from the United Provinces. In later years sons of old New Netherland families occupied on three occasions the highest office in the White House. Martin van Buren and two Roosevelts. Americans all! But of good Holland stock!

Holland's house was reduced to more modest proportions. In South Africa the former Dutch settlement, towards the end of the 18th century, took its fate in its own hands. In the far east the entire Malay Archipelago was seized by the English when after the French revolution, Holland, for a while, became a powerless instrument in the hands of France. But most of it was returned after the Netherlands, in 1815, re-entered the European scene as an independent and sovereign kingdom. And so the house, in that year, found its definite exterior, as we still know it today.

Its rooms extend over three continents: Europe, Asia and America; Holland proper, the Dutch East Indies and the Dutch West Indies. For almost a century and a quarter this structure has not materially changed. Not so the interior decoration. But that is another story.

47

IV. THE SPIRIT OF THE HOUSE

The Dutch character has sometimes been summed up as a queer mixture of obstinacy, tempered by common sense. And if this is correct, there were good reasons for it. A man who has to watch out all the time to prevent the sea from flooding and drowning him, has to be an obstinate person, or he would pack up and look for a less troublesome place elsewhere. A man who has to live behind dikes and on a rather small piece of soil with little or no useful minerals in it, has to use a lot of common sense to make both ends meet. His is not an easy life, and he may have a special liking for quarrelling with his immediate neighbour, as two extreme individualists, about all sorts of problems: matters theological, political, philosophical, artistic, economic and what not. It prevents his mind from getting rusty, and keeps him on the alert all the time. But in his dealings with the outside world he has always understood that this mind and his door had to be kept open to many things. He exchanged his merchandise, he exchanged ideas, he carried the goods of the world in his ships, he carried the thoughts of the world in his brain, and sometimes in his soul. A serious minded person, he, though by no means a saint, and in whose mentality the struggles of the past, against nature as well as against human enemies, have left their traces. But with a keen eye for the good things life and the world have to offer, and quite ready for a hearty laugh, even beneath the grey skies which his most famous 17th century painters cherished on canvas.

In no European country, it is said, has the character of the territory exercised so great an influence on the inhabitants as in the Netherlands. And on the other hand no people has so extensively modified the condition of its territory as the Dutch. They turned sea into land, land into canals, unruly streams into normalized rivers, inland lakes into meadows.

The low lands, between the estuaries of three great rivers, offering easy access to invaders, still possess specimens of the early convents and churches, strongholds of a new civilisation, built along the lines of that severe and forbidding Romanic style, the chief object of which seemed to be to keep, like fortresses, intruders out. Then, at the beginning of the 13th century, life in Holland begins to smile more easily. The less austere Gothic style, leaving more freedom to look out into the open from within, and admitting the outside world through larger windows, coincides with the art of bookprinting, widening man's horizon. The compass is invented, the world, explored by courageous seafarers, becomes larger and larger. New ideas originate, or, coming from abroad, find response. The Renaissance changes the intellectual and moral attitude of Europe and the Netherlands. New theories arise about the state and the church. The humanistic attitude springs from a yearning for a freeer expression of human self esteem. In the field of religion the Renaissance leads up to the Reformation for those who, for the first time, read the Bible with eyes enlightened by Humanism. And in the Netherlands the struggle against Spain for religious and political freedom becomes a manifestation of this same Renaissance, striving after self-emancipation; a great principle of which that gentle Dutch philosopher Erasmus had taught, and, which would find new

49

THE HOLLANDER IS AN INDIVIDUALIST:
8 MILLION KINGS IN THEIR OWN MIND
IN THEIR OWN HOME.

applications later, in England and America and, with all its yellow, black and white, in the French revolution.

It has been stated that Europe in a large measure owes the modern ideal of political liberty to that spirit of stubborn Dutch resistance, which broke the power of Spain: Holland's greatest contribution to the emancipation of mankind. The eighty years war steeled their energy, their self-reliance. In the year of their victory, 1648, the burghers of Amsterdam started constructing Jacob van Campen's famous town hall, today the palace of Queen Wilhelmina, a proud monument of a proud city, conceived in a period of triumphant feeling, tempered by certain fundamental traits of deeply rooted Dutch simplicity. It was the golden age of the Netherlands, of great statesmen like Frederick Henry, John de Witt, stadtholder William III, of great sailors like Tromp and De Ruyter, of great thinkers like Spinoza, jurists like Grotius, poets like Vondel, painters like Rembrandt, and the enterprising captains of industry, commerce and finance who directed their ships all over the world.

Then a reaction sets in. In the political and military sense their is a certain weakening. French styles and rationalism (Montesquieu, Voltaire, Rousseau) exert their influence. And finally, with the French revolution, Holland, for a short while, completely looses its balance, as well as its independence. But after Napoleon turns the revolutionary freedom into a forerunner of the totalitarian state, and before Waterloo wipes out Napoleon, Holland once more pulls itself together, to face, once more on its own strength, the confusing problems of the 19th and 20th centuries, the age of steam, electricity and surging scientific and technical development in general. The age of steel and concrete, of radio, motor cars, aviation, of motorized warfare and everything it implies on land, on the high seas and in the air. But also the age of educational and social ripening, evolution and strife, of political democracy, its blessings, its shortcomings and their consequences, the age of new faith, new efforts to penetrate into the meaning of life and death. The age of a new 'colonial style' in the administration and supervision of the millions of people in the Dutch possessions far east and west. The age of economic crises and the vital need to reorganize the natural ressources and talents of the country and its inhabitants so as to be able to weather the storms. The age of a serious try-out to create collective security by establishing international rules of conduct and a league of nations to observe and defend them. The age of the world war to end war and to make the world safe for democracy. The age of great confusions and disillusions. A crowded age, with room still for tireless new beginnings to build that never ending structure: the world of tomorrow.

V. RULES AND REGULATIONS

The national freedom, conquered on Spain, lost again to Napoleon, but retaken in 1813, was consolidated in the constitution of the new kingdom of the Netherlands, based on the principles of liberty of conscience, worship, freedom of the press, and political equality. The dominating power in the state was still vested in the monarch. After the separation and the secession in 1831 of the southern provinces, henceforth forming the independent kingdom of Belgium, and under the influence of the revolutionary movements in Europe of 1848, the fundamental law was amended that year, and constitutional, parliamentary government took a step forward. Ministers were now responsible to the States General. Gradually the franchise was extended to an increasing number of voters, and gradually political power shifted towards parliament. Until finally universal suffrage for both sexes over 25 years of age was achieved and a system of proportional representation introduced.

And so the long struggle for freedom ended in a complete emancipation of the Dutch people, collectively and individually. 350 Years were needed before the United Provinces, who took up arms against Spain, could become that full fledged democracy which is now building its future under the wise leadership of Queen Wilhelmina, daughter of that Orange dynasty which never failed, whenever called upon, to give its wisdom and services to the Dutch people, ever since the day when William the Silent united a handful of autonomous territories into a federated nation.

We have said before that the Dutch are and always have been

staunch individualists, with a natural tendency to disagree amongst themselves as long as they are not forced by circumstances to close their ranks against some common danger. Recent political history bears that out with some remarkable figures. At the general election of 1933 no less than 54 political parties or groups presented themselves to share the benefits of the system of proportional representation. It is a tribute to the common sense of the average voter that as many as 40 dropped out immediately, by failing to obtain enough votes for one single parliamentary mandate. Four years later, at the polls of 1937, self criticism and self correction bore fruit. The number of political rivals amongst the parties decreased to 20, of which only 10 succeeded to bring one or more representatives in parliament.

Still, for a comparatively small nation of 8 million inhabitants 10 parties seem quite a lot. But considering the fact that the nation was born in a war between two religions, and that religious problems have ever since remained the principal preoccupation of many, many Dutchmen, it is not so strange that today's political life and party politics should show the traces of such strong and living currents. And so, next to the principal political parties: Protestants, Roman Catholics, Liberals (on the decline after a long powerful reign), and Social Democrats, sub-divisions have occurred in many instances, and other groups, based on still further specialized religious and social conceptions have been added, besides the small Communist Party and, since a few years, the more noisy than convincing National Socialist Party which was built and acts faithfully along the lines of the mighty German pattern.

THERE ARE ROADS LIKE THIS......

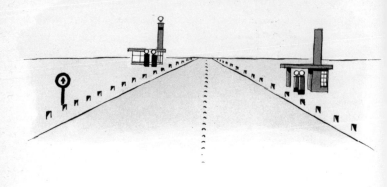

AND LIKE THAT

The presence of both extremes: communism and national socialism, two conceptions of kindred totalitarian regimes, is, in Holland and elsewhere, a serious warning that democracy must not be analytical or equitably representative only, but synthetical as well, and that government of the people, by the people and for the people, as Abraham Lincoln styled it at Gettysburg, must, if it does not want to perish from the earth, be able to concentrate the national forces by their own free will more effectively than the totalitarians try to accomplish through the abolishment of personal freedom in its most important and fundamental manifestations.

Here again the hereditary monarch, standing by right and intention *above* the parties, and embodying the continuity of the national interests, the national rights and the national duties, performs an invaluable function. The Kings and Queen of Holland have always lived up to that difficult position. When in September 1938, Queen Wilhelmina celebrated the fortieth anniversary of her accession to the throne, the greatest compliment a grateful nation could pay her, was the recognition that she had scrupulously fulfilled the task entrusted to her by the letter and the spirit of the constitution. Parties, political leaders, voters and even ministers of the crown may quarrel, disagree and fight each other with all the means at the disposal of a civilized society of free and thinking men and women, but the Queen thinks in terms of national synthesis, and acts accordingly: a permanent force, the keeper of the national conscience. And in times of crisis, when danger threatens the nation, behind revolutionary ambushes within, or in the international thunderclouds over the world at large, the people turn instinctively towards the descendent of the House of Orange, and like a flash party strife is forgotten and the 'sacred union', so elusive under normal circumstances, emanates from somewhere. As Mr. Neville Chamberlain stated the other day in a radio-speech: 'As a people we like to have our grumbles, but sometimes it is better to count our blessings.' A Dutchman might have said as much.

In the history of the Netherlands these moments occur again and again. And in our own times examples of it are not lacking. So in 1914, when the Dutch army marched to guard the frontiers to keep Holland out of the world war, and when even the socialists forgot their class-antagonism in order to become convinced patriots. So in November 1918 when the leader of those same socialists miscalculated the popular feeling and — somewhat ingenuously — announced his revolutionary intentions in parliament sufficiently in advance to give to government and the population a fair warning. And in a rush the nation prepared such energetic resistance that the revolution could be neatly nipped in the bud, and the whole affair ended with an unrivalled public demonstration of jubilant loyalty to the royal family. So again in February 1933, when in the East Indies a Dutch man-of-war fell into the hands of a rebellious crew, and a military bomb from the sky had to be used to suppress the mutiny. With a rude shock the nation awoke to the realization of how deeply and shamefully discipline and governmental authority had been allowed to sink and deteriorate. Again the people flocked around the throne. True, at the election, following these tragic events, no less than 54 parties came to the polls. But the government, at the special command of the Queen, was formed

THERE ARE CLASSICAL WINDMILLS,
BRAVING THE CENTURIES ....

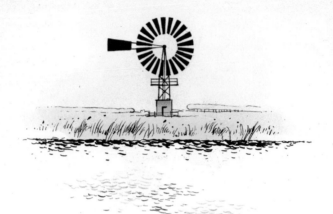

AND OTHERS, DONNING THE LATEST
STYLE~

on as broad a national basis as circumstances would permit. For the first time after long years of irreconcilable hostility between the liberals and progressives on the one hand, and the protestant and catholic parties on the other, the cleavage was bridged, and a national government came into being, with Dr Colijn, Holland's most experienced 'elder statesman', as its prime minister. Today he still captains the governmental team, but after four years the revolutionary scare is almost forgotten and after the new popular verdict of the usual periodical elections of 1937, the governmental basis has been narrowed down again to something considerably less than national-wide.

Can the nation afford as much, or rather, as little? The problems of national defense, of economic crisis, of social legislation, of fighting unemployment, of financial readjustment are serious, like in any other country, and require the greatest possible concentration of national energy and national goodwill. And in a world where, for the moment, democracy is on the defensive, a country where freedom is still cherished as dearly as it was in the days of the founding fathers, must be ready for action, internally and externally. With united forces.

The nation as a whole realizes this full well. In its political expressions it may seem to accentuate the differences of opinion and of principle which are at the basis of their divided parties and groups, but beyond party loyalty their exists a growing understanding of the collective needs of the country and the people. Again the Queen has found the words to interpret the feelings which are stirring the heart of the nation. In radio speeches she has explained on more than one occasion the imperative necessity for 'moral and spiritual rearmament' in the outside world as well as at home. The necessity for mutual understanding and mutual help. And not with words alone.

History repeats itself. And if one is permitted to make one guess, it is this: that whenever the water will rise again as high as the lips of the eight million Dutch individualists, these low-landers, who know what rising water means, will be found once more to stand together, with unshakable faith in their destinies, and conscious of the last and vital warning: to be or not to be.

As it was in the beginning. As it is now. As it will be, as long as free men live on free soil.

VI. A HOME AMONGST NEIGHBOURS

We must revert anew to the Dutchman behind his dike. He had to build dikes and dams, literally and figuratively speaking. Dikes against the water, and dikes against possible other invaders with a roving eye on a wealthy nation, occupying strategically extremely important positions in Europe and Asia, and, to a lesser degree in America. During their struggle for independence and the years of consolidation the Dutch needed some active allies once in a while, and consequently had to take a most lively part in the political games of the world. There was a time when The Hague was considered one of the busiest centres of European diplomatic activity. However, once the nation had been put on a sound and practical basis, and became completely engaged in the gigantic task to develop—with its 8 million homelanders—not only the mother country, but the East and West Indies as well—a total land area of about 800.000 sq. miles (as compared to the 3000.000 sq. miles of continental U.S.A.) with a total population of about 69.000.000 — the words of another founding father, far away in the new world, were remembered: Beware of foreign entanglements! The spirit of George Washington.

Quite naturally so. Here they were, having built their world on several shores, losing some, gaining some, and consolidating all they kept into a strong and modern commonwealth. With their realm situated in three continents, bordering on the North Sea, the Atlantic and the Pacific, with long and vulnerable lines of communication to maintain, and surrounded almost everywhere by large and mighty neighbours, they had to avoid

63

quarrels and too close friendships alike. It would be foolishness to mix with the political aspirations of the big powers, thereby deliberately risking to be drawn into other people's conflicting interests, in which Holland could at best hope to play the role of a very junior partner, whose career would decidedly not be foremost in the minds of the seniors.

Holland's responsibility, towards its own people and the world at large, demanded another line of conduct: To be— as Queen Wilhelmina in one of her recent public speeches so clearly and rightly expressed it—nobody's follower and nobody's agressor. To promote, wherever and whenever possible the peace of the world, which happens to be a vital need for the free existence of the far flung Dutch commonwealth. To watch out carefully and conscienciously that the strategic key-positions of its territories in Europe and Asia, at the cross-roads of economical, political, military and naval power-lines of strong neighbouring countries, will never be abused for the agressive designs of possible malevolent outsiders.

It is not by mere chance that the mightiest nations of the world who, if they should choose to, could by their combined superior forces, wipe the kingdom of the Netherlands off the face of the earth as an independent nation, recognized, at the Congress of Vienna in 1815, the significance of a viable Dutch nation. In supporting Holland, in Europe and overseas, they served their own interests. They realized that Holland and the Dutch East and West Indies, in the hands of a bigger power, might easily and at any time become a dangerous obstacle in the international path of others, or a base of attack against adjacent territories, important trade routes or naval lines of communi-

IN A LITTLE DUTCH TOWN

cation; whereas they also knew that Holland, once firmly established in its possessions, would cherish no dreams for further expansion at somebody else's expense.

Looked at from this angle the support given to the Dutch seemed to be a sound international political investment. The balance of power in western Europe and in the far east, the peace around the North Sea and in the Pacific Ocean, the safety in Central American waters, so near the Panama-Canal, are matters of vital interest to several of the bigger powers. For all these reasons, they could hardly remain indifferent if the independence and integrity of Holland in Europe, Asia or America, should be seriously threatened or impaired. For there would be much more at stake than Dutch democracy, born and raised in that historical cradle of political liberty, which inspired others, and not in the last place the United States of America. The political and strategical equilibrium of the world would painfully be disturbed if the keys of Holland should disappear in foreign pockets.

And so Holland's foreign policy is and must be a policy of peace and independence, free from political alliances or military pacts or agreements. It was only when president Woodrow Wilson wrote the chapter concerning the League of Nations into the peace treaty of Versailles, that the Dutch nation, welcoming to new life those great and noble principles which their compatriot Grotius had unsuccessfully proclaimed 300 years earlier, consented to align itself with most of the other nations of the world in order to establish a system of collective security. A system, so they hoped, to be founded on political justice and international law, and on that orderly freedom, tolerance and mutual respect, which more or less succesfully they had tried to apply in their own dealings with each other and with the world. Henceforward Holland stood committed to collective action, in which its own councillors would no longer be able under *all* circumstances to take final diplomatic decisions without others having some say in the matter. It meant a change and a sacrifice. But the ultimate aim seemed worth it.

Again Queen Wilhelmina interpreted the deepest convictions of the Dutch people when, on the 17th of May 1933, she telegraphed her reply to the message which president Franklin D. Roosevelt had circulated to the heads of the states of the world, to tell them of his views on war and peace: 'Our nation—Her Majesty stated—in whose name I speak, detests war. It would, without a doubt, resist agression, but it looks upon war with horror. Just as it condemns provocation and attack amongst citizens, it condemns provocation and attack amongst nations. It believes the time has come for the community of nations to prove with acts, that they are firmly resolved to reject the right of the strongest as their ultimate and highest standard. Peaceful settlement is the only method to make up national disputes. I know of no reason why peaceful settlement should not be the only method to arrange international quarrels. My people are strongly convinced that, in order to achieve these aims, far reaching disarmament will be necessary now. For continued armament must lead to an armaments race, and, as painful but all too soon forgotten experience has shown, to inevitable war.'

These words were the royal expression of what the entire nation believed, and feels today. Yet the Dutch, who also believe in the laws of nature but must fight its water, have learned sufficient history to know by common sense that they must be realists as well as idealists. And when the events of the last five or six years made it quite clear that the League of Nations — which can not possibly be stronger than its individual member states, put together, permit its collectivity to be — miserably fell short of what one had dreamt, hoped and expected, the Dutch government together with the Scandinavian states, Belgium and Switzerland, resolutely reclaimed the full right to decide for itself in each and every future case, as to whether, and to what extent, it would take part in whatever collective action the League might want to embark upon.

The great principles outlined by Grotius and Wilson still hold good. But as long as the world is not ready to abide by them, a small nation with a big job must be careful not to entangle itself in the wires of a complicated piece of international machinery that does not work; especially when others seem to monopolize the strings.

No one can tell what the future holds in store. Perhaps one day the world will come to the conclusion that there is indeed no reason — as Queen Wilhelmina observed — why peaceful settlement should not become the only method for dealing with international disputes. Perhaps some day, the League of Nations will actually become that universal council of states against whose combined power no one will ever dare to launch agressive violence. When that day comes, the land of Grotius will undoubtedly want to reconsider its position and its policy. But in the interval it must jealously retain the right to safeguard its vital interests, which are identical with those of peace, freedom and tolerance; and to safeguard them according to the realities of each separate occasion.

During the Washington Conference for the reduction of naval armaments on the basis of political pacification around the Chinese problem, Holland, being present as one of the Pacific powers, obtained in February 1922 identical written promises from the governments of the United States, Japan, England and France, in which each of these four countries declared itself 'firmly resolved to respect the rights of the Netherlands in relation to their insular possessions in the region of the Pacific Ocean'. In Europe, Holland's immediate big neighbours, England and Germany, have repeatedly declared their intention to respect Dutch territory, Dutch independence and Dutch neutrality. Both England and Germany maintain a vital interest in that none of the two shall use the lowlands as a naval, military or air-base against the other. As for the West Indies, it seems unlikely that the historical Monroe doctrine would not become involved in case some strong non-American power should try to undo the work of well-nigh three centuries.

And so the house of Holland stands watchfully amongst the other houses, some big, some small, some like steel fortresses, some like concrete bee-hives full of airplanes. And the Dutch look on and out and keep their powder dry. There have been times when the family seemed to become careless about the shutters and the bolts of the front door. But the events of the last four or five years have made them think twice and act fast. The visitor who now crosses their threshold will find them busily mending the rusty locks, cleaning the old shotgun and ordering a thing or two to keep out trespassers, if need be. Economically and culturally speaking they may still cherish the old ideal of the open door, inasmuch as reciprocal feeling and conduct elsewhere will permit them, but in matters of safety on the premises their house must be their impregnable castle, if Holland, and all it stands for, is to remain a zone of peace and goodwill towards all in its exposed position on what a Frenchman once gracefully pictured as 'the balcony of Europe'.

VII. THE INTENSIVE DUTCH GARDEN

A 19th century Dutch poet once, in a depressed mood and probably on a rainy day, wrote down a hymn of ire against his 'land of dung and fog, of chilly dew and damp.' All of that Holland, like many other countries, undoubtedly is and has. But it also has wide and mighty skies and quite a dose of sunshine: a gift of nature. And fertile fields, green pastures, cities large and small, teeming with industrial, commercial, cultural and artistic life: a gift of man. Still, it must be admitted that they picked no *easy* spot to settle, these early Dutchmen of two thousand years ago. Today fully one quarter of the country consists of drained marshes and 'polders': lakes turned into land behind dams, and even sea turned into soil behind dikes. Fertile soil, quite often, but for that they had to wage an exhaustive war with the water. Where hilly regions were found free of charge, chiefly in the south and middle east, the soil consisted mainly of sand and gravel and sometimes of peat. Not a very convenient place to make a living, unless one is prepared to think hard and work harder.

Yet, or perhaps just because of that, the Dutch have turned out to be a prolific and healthy people, tackling a difficult job in good cheer, and quite successfully so. After they had found their definite political and national bearings, there was a rapid growth of population, resulting not so much from a high birth rate as from a low and steadily declining death rate: with 8,8 per 1000 inhabitants now the lowest in fact of all the nations in the world. In a hundred years time, from 1830 to 1930, the population of the motherland more than trebled, increasing from $2^1/_2$ million to almost 8 million, and the latter mark has now again been left well behind. According to some calculations, the population-figures in years to come may stabilize in the neighbourhood of 12 million. How to house and feed such numbers on the comparatively narrow strip of European Holland, presents a problem which keeps the best minds of the country constantly at work.

To do that the soil, what there is of it, must be constantly improved so that it may yield the fullest, most useful and most profitable returns. And if peaceful territorial expansion is possible, by new conquests of sea-bottom, many Dutchmen feel now, as they did in the early centuries of our Christian era, that it *should* be done, even though, strictly economically speaking, the costprice of the new land, if left alone, would send farmers rents skyrocketing. But then again, the soil is eternal, and no one can foretell whether the present agricultural crisis will last for ever, whereas it is quite certain that Holland's house will need a larger living room before long. And so the great inland Zuyder Zee is slowly but surely vanishing from the map. Already modern, mechanical farming outfits have harvested crops where at one time, not more than 25 years ago, fishermen sailed their boats full of living haul.

But territorial inward extension in Holland must necessarily be limited. And since there cannot be *more* soil all the time, the existing soil must be bettered as much and as rapidly as modern natural science, agricultural chemistry and perfected tools will permit. Within the Dutch frontiers extensive farming has ceased to exist long, long ago. The Dutch farmer, in agriculture, cattle breeding, horticulture, floriculture and the nursery-

TURNING THE ZUYDER ZEE INTO LAND:

AS IT WAS IN 1918

business in general, has become a master of intensive treatment of the soil, and equally intensive production methods. He lives in a small country. For lack of suitable space he cannot migrate, even if he were less conservatively attached to his particular piece of land. Consequently he must find the solution of his problem with the help of active science and economics, cooperative purchasing. cooperative marketing, diversified farming etc.

The government lends him a cordial and helping hand. It provides agricultural schools, scientific research, supervision and controlling stations. It has recognized the extremely important social, economic and commercial significance of the farmer, the steady citizen, rooted in his soil, faithful to fundamental values which he has learned from his daily contact with the eternal laws of nature. About 20% of the working population of Holland tills two thirds of the national soil in one way or another, or uses it as grassland for cattle breeding and milk production, which, in turn, has become the basis of an extremely important dairy industry. And in the export trade of the country the farmer, the cattle breeder, the dairy man, the fruit- and vegetable-grower and the nursery man provide, directly or indirectly, something between 25 and 30% of its total value.

Intensive agriculture! Where soil is scarce, one builds sky-scrapers like on Manhattan Island or cultivates deeply like in Holland. It means that Holland has left to larger countries the mass production of wheat, corn, beef-on-the-hoof, cattle-fodder etc., for all of which the huge prairies and fields of America, Canada, and other 'wide open spaces', less densely populated

74

TURNING THE ZUYDER ZEE INTO LAND:

AS IT LOOKED IN 1934

AS IT IS TODAY~

than Holland with its 640 inhabitants per sq. mile (compared to 43 per sq. mile in the United States), are in a much better position. He who cultivates a small garden prefers to buy these things abroad, using them as raw material to be refitted and graded up to something else, into which the acquired skill and workmanship of the specialized Dutchman can be worked on a sound economic basis.

And so they turn fodder into Friesian Holsteins, high class breeding cattle, or again into 'blue ribbon' milk cows; they turn cows into milk and butter and cheese; they turn corn into pork, and pork into the bacon for the world's breakfast tables. They buy foreign fertilizers to change them into excellent fruit and vegetables, roses and tulips and every other kind of flower, which go by airmail to the far corners of Europe, and, if they are bulbs, to the far corners of the earth. Quality, quality, must be the aim of those who cannot compete with the immense mass productions of others.

And quality it shall be! The government and private initiative have seen to it that most of these products are placed under special control. Holland's garden wants to smell sweet under the critical noses of its international customers . . .

Of course the economic world crisis, the disturbed international political situation and the resulting tendency in many countries towards an artificial and costly self-sufficiency within its own frontiers, have played their tricks also in this intensive Dutch garden. Foreign doors have suddenly been slammed into the face of the Dutch farmer and his colleagues of the kindred trades. And so a topsy turvy world forces the gardeners of Holland to make room in their fields for at least some of the things they cannot any longer buy abroad, because the people abroad have decided to make their own cheese and butter, and grow their own flowers and vegetables. Their own, even if perhaps more costly and less perfect than the specialized products of these Dutchmen who acquired a special skill for this sort of work, just as other people in other countries acquired special knowledge for the manufacture of motorcars, safety razors or heavy artillery.

Yes, perhaps less perfect, and more costly, *but their own!* That seems to be the highest wisdom of our times. By applying this wisdom, every country contributes to the general crisis for each and every one of us. So governments rush out with a dole for the unemployed and subsidies and all kinds of protection for all the people and all the trades that have got into one and the same trouble. And in return for help the governments demand the right to regulate business and put it entirely in chains. And that again makes it more difficult for everybody else. And so they all run around in one common, endless and extremely vicious circle.

As Alice in Wonderland once meditated: If we could only grow big enough or small enough to fit into all this . . .

VIII FISHPOND AND BOATHOUSE

If it had not been for the modest herring, moving for reasons of taste to the North Sea from the Baltic, where the water was gradually beginning to lose its saline constituents, the history of Holland might have taken a different course. For it was the herring that made the Dutch go down to the sea in ships. And when a fisherman from Zeeland, William Beukelszoon, discovered the art of how to cure the fish, so that it might be preserved and stored away in casks for long term trading purposes, the basis had been laid for a regular import- and export traffic along the sea routes, and simultaneously for the beginnings of the Dutch merchant marine. Hence the fishpond and the boathouse, in our story, belong together.

For the herring fisheries led to commercial exchanges, from which resulted the grain trade. And out of the grain trade, carrying Baltic wheat in Dutch ships to Lisbon, that famous market for far-eastern goods, came the rediscovery by the Dutch of the sea route to India. And out of this rediscovery grew Holland's colonial possessions, now absorbed as integral parts into the commonwealth of the Netherlands. Without them, Holland would be a small nation without further ado. With them, it is a small European nation with a large empire and a heavy responsibility of world wide dimensions. So it can hardly be denied that the 20th century Dutchman owes the ancient herring an earnest vote of thanks.

Since the Dutchman's herring finds its final destination for 75% on foreign plates, the least the Hollanders could do was to place it under efficient control by the government, so as to

A MODEST VILLAGE, THAT SHOULD HAVE BEEN A PLACE
OF PILGRIMAGE: BIERVLIET, WHERE THE INVENTOR
OF THE ART OF CURING THE DUTCH HERRING, WILLIAM
BEUKELSZOON, WAS BORN FIVE CENTURIES AGO —
HE SHOWED THE WAY TO THE DUTCH MERCANTILE MARINE

guarantee that it would face the ultimate consumer in perfect condition. Just as if it had been a cow or an Edam cheese or a pound of Dutch butter. Quality production again! And what goes for the herring also goes for his friends, the halibut, the cod and the haddock, the sole, the turbot and the flat fish, the anchovy and the shrimp, the oyster and the mussel, and for the 'dramatis personae' of the inner-fisheries: the salmon, perch and pike and the slippery eel. Private initiative and government supervision have resulted in better boats (there are about 3400 of them), fisherman schools, better police-measures on the high sea, chemical, hydrographical and bio-logical research stations, scientific development of better specimen, etc. A very modern outfit for a very ancient trade. The old sailing boats—a famous Dutch playwright, Herman Heyermans, built a social drama around them—are now sur-rendering their places to the less picturesque but more efficient motor-schooners. But what remains unchanged (how long?) are the quaint and colourful costumes which the natives of many fisherman's villages along the North Sea shore and even along the remaining Zuyder Zee shores still like to don, oblivious to our standardized up to date fashion which makes all of us look exactly alike. Apart from that, the fisherman's trade, one of the very oldest in the country, has put on 20th century attire. Even the economic crisis has touched it, with a quite modern sledge hammer . . .

Down to the sea in ships! And down in ships to the far cor-ners of the world, bringing home the merchandise (and the bacon!) of distant shores, carrying goods of, from and for

BULBFIELDS

others as well as themselves, offering to others their age-long Dutch experience of rough seas and bad weather and of exploring unknown regions, and sailing their vessels with an unusual margin of safety, which, by the way, procured them—in later times—such favourable insurance rates at Lloyds of London, that they could afford to be more reasonable than many others.

'Navigare necesse est.' Plutarch's words might have been coined by and for the Hollanders of all times. Without that their little corner of clay, sand and gravel would never have allowed them to subsist. They had to go out and discover additional sources of materials and income, which they could use directly or exchange with other countries for the goods they needed. Even now they have to import considerably more than they can export to foreign markets. In 1937 a little more than 25% of the value of Dutch imports remained unbalanced by exports. In order to make up for the difference they must find their income elsewhere. The returns on their foreign and Dutch East Indian investments, economic disturbances permitting, can fill part of the gap. Services rendered to others must do the rest: by carrying foreign goods and passengers in Dutch ships—or in Dutch airplanes all over Europe and the West Indies, or to the far east, for that matter—by showing the sights of Holland in three continents to the tourists of the world, or any other scenery accessible to Dutch mariners.

'Navigare necesse est.' For the Netherlands perhaps more than for many others. And when, in the 15th and the 16th century, it became customary in many maritime states to claim exclusive sovereignty over seas and even oceans, it was a Dutch jurist, Grotius, who wrote his 'Mare Liberum' in protest, maintaining that the sea should *not* be made the property of any state. A principle to which, in England, John Selden, in 1635, immediately opposed his 'Mare Clausum'.

The freedom of the seas, in times of war especially is still an unsolved problem, as delicate as it is dangerous. International rules pertaining to neutral shipping, the right of search and capture, conditional and unconditional contraband, have been broken often, and variously interpreted by many who were, directly or indirectly, parties to armed conflicts. During the American Civil War England and Lincoln's America almost clashed over such prickly points. In our own times submarine warfare—as neutral shipping painfully experienced during the world war—has complicated these matters still further. But the sound principle which Grotius defended will always be cherished and carried on by the Dutch. The high sea must not be any-body's private property. It must be free as a wide and natural road to prosperity for everybody's peaceful enterprise. And whoever has the power to 'rule the waves', should rule them in the name of liberty.

With more than a thousand ships Holland sails the seven seas. But it also sails less fickle and less freakish waters. Having conquered its soil from bogs and marshes and lakes, it had to drain the water away into canals and rivers, and in this manner it combined the reclamation of new land with the establishment of new waterways: the roads for the cheapest form of transpor-tation. The old fashioned sailing barges and tow-boats with a horse or a couple of men at the end of the rope are still to be seen, though perhaps in a less romantic, dramatic and musical

84

style than that of the famous Wolga-boatmen. But here also the motorized traffic is rapidly replacing an older technical equipment.

Steel and machinery and oil and gasoline are the materials which keep the Dutch shipyards busily engaged. Of course, the omnipresent economic crisis has forced Holland, along with almost every other country, to face the intricate problem of the coordination of rail-, road- and water-traffic, since for all three combined, there seem to be too many carriers in relation to the available freight of both passengers and merchandise. And so for all competitors, the soup is getting thin. But then, that will hardly be news to anybody, in whatever corner of our slightly unbalanced earth, where the time is by no means the only thing that's out of joint.

IX. THE INDUSTRIOUS WORKSHOP

Take a little bit of land and a lot of water. Pick it in such a way that even the most indiscreet detective could discover no other minerals than coal and salt. Recruit your inhabitants from amongst men who will increase their numbers quicker than their acres of cultivable soil, and to a greater extent than agriculture and fisheries together can absorb and feed. Conclusion: The rest must go in for trade, transportation and industry, or bust.

That is exactly what happens in Holland today. In the last forty years—since Queen Wilhelmina ascended the throne—the population of the Netherlands (in Europe) increased by 70%, but the cultivated area only by 16%. This, amongst other reasons, drove many of those who should have been, by family tradition, farmers or fishermen, into the factories, commerce and transportation. In those forty years the farming-fishing quota of the total number of Dutchmen employed fell from 33 to 20%, whereas the factory quota rose from 32 to 39% and the trade and transport legion from 16 to 23%. Of course the economic crisis has done its unpleasant bit in an allround fashion. But that only confirmed the national problem: creating jobs and incomes for a steadily growing family, living in one and the same house which has reached its limit of expansion, and in a garden where only some can find enough to do to make it worth while.

Fortunately the farmer and the fisherman produce, in their line, more than the family can consume. The surplus is either used as raw material for industrial purposes (dairy) or exported

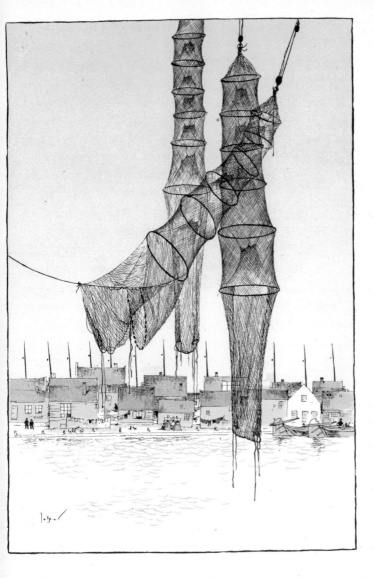

FISHING TACKLE

directly to foreign markets in exchange for finished articles, semi-manufactured goods or raw materials. These last two can then be put into final or semi-final shape in Dutch factories, and used either for home consumption or for re-export.

In this way it becomes possible for a country without most of the important minerals, to give employment to almost twice as many industrial workers as the historical occupations of agriculture and the fisheries can take care of. So that industry figures with 57°/₀ in the total export-value. On the other hand this complicated process of importing raw material, improving it, finishing it, exporting it in exchange for other goods, or, vice versa, exporting agricultural raw material in exchange for finished articles, keeps also traders, bankers and carriers busy. Add to this the special geographical position of Holland, Europe's balcony, with its rivers and canals, its sea-ports and railroads with direct international connections, and acting as inlets and outlets, not only for the Netherlands, but for the north western European hinterland altogether, and the fundamental structure of this very industrious workshop will emerge.

There are, of course, the Dutch East Indies, producers of many minerals and tropical agricultural merchandise of which the world needs sufficient quantities to enable those in control of the mines and plantations of the Malaysian Archipelago to invest the proceeds into other enterprises and other goods, thereby making up for things absent within the confines of the Dutch commonwealth. Without the Indies, Holland would certainly not be Holland as we know it now. But without Holland the Dutch East Indies would almost as certainly have become somebody's private hunting field, with no rights of its own to exert, but only with rights to surrender, instead of being an emancipated part of a world wide realm. Just as it would have been impossible for the primitive technical and economical equipment of the East Indies to create the amount of wealth which, thanks to the leadership, the capital, the trade relations and skill of the Dutch, now forms the firm basis for the sound educational, social and political development of these 60 million Asiatic natives.

It is clear that under these circumstances a reasonably free international exchange of goods is of vital interest to the commonwealth of the Netherlands, and its individual members. And it is also quite natural that Holland's free trade policy, as written in the tariff law of 1862, has witnessed and promoted a steady industrial growth, on the foundations of an important and natural agricultural production, a transportation system of international scope, and against a strong and generally healthy financial background, showing the contours of the proud city of Amsterdam as one of the impressive money-markets of the world.

From 1862 to 1923, for more than sixty years, this liberal policy could remain practically unchanged. What Holland needed most, was admitted duty-free, what it needed less fell under a general duty of 5% ad valorem. Apart from that there were no restrictions or hindrances on imports. And as long as foreign countries were prepared to take in exchange the agricultural products of Holland and the Indies, or the finished goods, made from foreign semi-manufactured or raw materials, the world seemed rather a jolly good place.

The world, however, refused to remain jolly and good. The

economic consequences of the peace treaties of 1919, which Mr Keynes foresaw so clearly when no one else believed him, unsettled the atmosphere like an oncoming thunderstorm. In 1923 the collapse of the German Mark forced Holland to put up a first barrier to prevent the market from getting drowned in German goods. The ad valorem duty advanced from 5 to 8°/₀. Not very serious yet. Other countries had meanwhile begun to reinforce their commercial armaments, with high tariffs, fighting tariffs, import-quota systems, currency-manipulation, government export subsidies, economic protection disguised as sanitary control, and all the other weapons, bare or camouflaged, which today we have learned to regard as the norms of 1939. The result was, and had to be, that countries who would no longer buy abroad, could no longer sell abroad, and that—though also through price-falls—the world value of international exports and imports fell considerably, each from about 35 billion of gold dollars in 1929 to about 13 billion in 1936, while the total value of Dutch imports over the same period decreased from more than 1 billion gold dollars in 1929 to about 350 millions in 1936. Exports, on a somewhat lower scale, followed the same downward trend.

In vain pleaded the Netherlands government in several international economic conferences in Geneva, London and elsewhere, for a return to common sense, to a more natural division of labor in the world, to a freeer exchange of goods, capital and services, to a lowering of the tariff walls, to a more generous application of the most favoured nation clause in trade treaties. In vain tried Holland to set an example with more than words, words, words, by concluding with Belgium the socalled Ouchyconvention, aiming at a gradual lowering of tariffs, on a basis of reciprocity, and offering, but also restricting, the advantages thereof to such countries as would be willing to do as much. The effort stranded on the rock of a British protest against what was called an infringement of the most favoured nation principle. But this principle had been broken over and over again, by all sorts of discriminations and by all sorts of nations, whether by means of 'imperial preference' or by any other name.

The real tragedy began after England, in September 1931, went off the gold standard. In the general confusion that followed throughout the world, Holland alone could not keep its door wide open. Import-quotas were introduced, the government was authorized to make clearing-treaties if and when necessary. The ad valorem tariff was raised from 8 to 10%. The possibility to resort to economic discrimination in certain cases, or to economic reprisals, was opened by law, further power to apply protective import duties was delegated to the government. The ad valorem tariff further rose from 10 to 12%, and finally, but not until the dollar had followed the pound in its farewell to the gold standard, and the French frank and many other currencies had followed both pound and dollar, the Dutch guilder, one of the very last defenders of the inviolability of a custom-honoured medium of exchange, in September 1936, gave way. And even that was not enough. In matters of economic protection it never is. Higher the tariff rose, up to 20% for certain goods, but still remaining well below the dizzy hights of so many foreign walls.

Economic self defence! And like the other means of protection in other fields: armies, guns, warships, warplanes, it will not end there. For every restrictive measure somewhere, invites a counter-measure somewhere else. And in the long run the result can only be a general impoverishment for each and everyone.

A New Deal, in the sense of an economic pacification of the world, is urgently needed. Perhaps no nation is more convinced of that than Holland, whose national economy can only come to full bloom in a world where commercial *exchange* is considered as a blessing instead of a pest. For that reason every serious and honest effort to promote a general reduction of armaments, be they cannons or trade barriers, may be certain of Dutch support. The recent trade treaty with the U.S.A. containing a number of mutual tariff lowerings shows once more a certain analogy in the outlook of both nations. Indeed, the industrious workshop of Holland's house greatly dislikes to function with its doors and windows closed. It much prefers a salty breeze on the premises. So does the garden.

Nevertheless it functions, and as well as can be expected under the circumstances. In a world full of locked doors, barricaded routes, no-tresspassing-signs, closed frontiers, crippled money, artificial economy and unfair competition, it manages to build ships, radio's, furniture, houses, electric lamps, and even motorcars; it manufactures artificial silk, sugar mills and many other kinds of heavy machinery; it has world famous diamond-cutting establishments, important chemical industries, it makes shoes and clothes, and textiles and cigars and rubber goods, it has some of the best equipped coalmines of the world, and one of the world's largest oil-concerns, with its industrial, commercial and transport ramifications all over the globe, has its headquarters in the centre of Holland's activities.

It is impossible to give a complete list. Nor is this necessary for obtaining a clear picture of how a small nation manages to do a big job in rough weather. To be sure, the family is not always agreed as to the best means to keep the home fires burning. And it is not very pleasant to have to admit that something like 5°/₀ of the inhabitants are unable to find normal and renumerative work. And so there is a great deal of discussion—pro and con—about all kinds of reorganizations; more government control, more managed economy, more arable land and accelerated industrialization to absorb the unemployed, more public money into private enterprise with or without unbalancing the national budget, etc. But to every 'more' advocated by some, a 'less' is opposed by others.

To Americans that will sound familiar. But then, in the restless search for the most workable economic, social and political means to promote that beckoning 'pursuit of happiness' of which the Declaration of Independence spoke a century and a half ago, we are all members of one great human family.

The family quarrels inclusive.

Equatorial Holland, far from the grey skies of north western Europe, baking in the tropical sun of eastern Asia and Middle and South America, forms the heritage of Dutch commercial enterprise in the 16th and 17th centuries. If Holland is the 'balcony' of Europe, the Dutch East and West Indies are the 'sun-porches' of Holland. We have told in a previous chapter how Holland's house felt an urgent need to build new rooms. It is quite certain that these early traders had not the slightest intentions of carrying western civilization into the primitive unknown. They were out for gain, commercial gain, and to fight their European enemies, the Spaniards and the Portuguese, in their own overseas hunting grounds. Europe was far too much occupied with the Renaissance, its religious and political wars, and very cruel wars at that, to have much breath left for an ethical essay on the dark skinned natives of the Malayan and American shores.

And so the foundations of a colonial empire were laid according to the prevailing codes of those rather rough-and-tumble times. The directors of the Dutch East and West India Companies were no better and no worse than their contemporaries. They were hard fighters and hard businessmen, and their foreign competitors were just as hard, if not harder. Americans, who can read in their own and not so very distant history about long wars between 'pale faces' and 'red skins'; who had to fight a civil war that slavery might be abolished; who still run 'Jim Crow cars' below the Mason and Dixon line, and who are still obliged to suppress occasional lynching practices, will understand that the Dutch colonists of 300 years ago were not exactly—and could not possibly be—soft spoken up-lifters, but strong minded persons, liable to make all the mistakes of people who must learn how to rule other people, but who were learning their lessons, slowly but surely.

It took three centuries. But thereafter a Javanese woman of noble birth, Kartini, could freely admit in her 'Letters of a Javanese Princess': 'It may sound strange, but it is nevertheless a fact that you Europeans have taught me to love my own land and people. Instead of estranging us from our native land, our European education has brought us nearer to it, has opened our hearts to our beauties and also to the needs of our people and to their weaknesses.'

That such a tribute could be paid to Dutch administration, that such a tremendous evolution could take place, must have been the result of common sense as well as of new ethical norms. Holland governing an overseas archipelago with an area equalling that of half non Russian Europe; 8 million Hollanders dealing with 60 million natives, such a state of affairs would be inconceivable if, in one way or another, the goodwill had not been won of the indigenous population (or rather populations, for in the Dutch East Indies more than 130 different native tribes and clans live together).

This result could only be achieved by wisely allotting to the natives a generous share of home rule and self administration on the basis however of certain general principles of fairness, order and loyalty to the supreme authority of the Queen of the Netherlands and Her Majesty's government. Today there are about 300 heterogeneous self-ruling territories in the Dutch

East Indies, supervised by the Dutch Civil Service, and, at the top, by the Dutch governor general. The need for administrative coordination in this multitude of more or less autonomous groups, and the wish to give the people an opportunity to take part, through their spokesmen, in the government of provinces, districts and local units, brought provincial and local self-governing bodies into being, with both European and native representation. To top off, the Dutch government in 1918 instituted a central advisory 'People's Council', which has now 61 members, 30 of whom are natives, partly appointed by the governor general, partly elected by the local councils. Through this method of representation — free government adapted to oriental conditions and political capacity — the voice of the Dutch East Indies may or must express itself on all matters of public interest.

It is not the purpose of this story to explain in detail the machinery of the Dutch East Indian government. It merely wants to show that those on the sun-porch of Holland's house completely changed their status of servility for that of junior partners in the family, enjoying the advantages of the well organized life of an old and experienced firm, with an international position which the Indies, left to their heterogeneous self, could never hope to attain or maintain. The disappearance of the central authority which keeps the 130 clans and tribes — many even with languages of their own — and their 300 self-ruling territories rallied around the principle of 'united with the Netherlands we stand, divided amongst ourselves we fall', would condemn these parts to unavoidable disintegration, which, in turn, would undoubtedly lead to foreign interventions, quite likely to be less well disposed towards the native rights and interests than Holland can well afford to be after three centuries of political and administrative understanding, schooling and achievement in the far east.

Exploitation is over. Education is in full swing, and its result must necessarily be to equip the native population with the knowledge, the technical means and an economic structure through which their chances of self-assertion will gradually improve. By amendment to the Netherlands constitution the Dutch East Indies, in 1922, very formally ceased to be 'colonies' and became an integral part of the commonwealth of the Netherlands. The object of Dutch rule henceforth is to let the Indies look after themselves in as large a measure as the total interests of the realm will allow. It is only natural that the process is a slow one, the educational task that goes with it being as colossal as it is costly. The great native masses have first to be acquainted with the essentials of every-day knowledge: reading, writing, hygiene, modernized agricultural methods, systemetical household finance, in order to prepare them for their task in a surrounding world, highly technical, highly organized and highly specialized in almost all its activities. If they want to mix and deal with the world at large, they must learn to keep up with the businesslike pace of that world. The obstacles to be overcome can perhaps be fathomed when it is realized that some 94% of the 60 million natives are still unable to express themselves on paper.

Starting with the introduction of native village schools, this very old and very large world had to be awakened to face a

THE TWENTIETH CENTURY IN HOLLAND

THE TWENTIETH CENTURY IN HOLLAND'S TROPICS

new one, in which it wants to play its part. It takes time and endurance to cover these enormous grounds. But already, on the upper end of the ladder the educated native can obtain his college degree at the School of Engineering in Bandung, or the Law School and the School of Medicine in Batavia. Between these extremes a long line of educational efforts and institutions spans. And so it goes along the entire educational front. Primitive, haphazard methods of food-production (especially rice) have to be reorganized into a regular system of production, storage, crop-financing, and liberating the native farmer, often without any power of economical or intellectual resistance, from the clutches of local usurers. Simple forms of credit- and saving-facilities have to be devised and patiently explained to the ignorant native, who, thus far, simply neglected to protect himself against periods of complete poverty and hunger.

Modern medical science has also to conquer endless superstition and prejudice in the native mind before it can enlist his support in the fight to save his race from tropical diseases like the plague, leprosy, Asiatic cholera, malaria, beri beri, smallpox etc. In an age of industrialization, the indolent farmhand has to be transformed into a man who can handle industrial tools and machines. And so the primitive native village school is the gate to a long road flanked by technical, financial, medical and other institutions, each and every one of them a milestone along the rising curve of native development.

Here, indeed, is a New Deal, helping the native to set his house in order. A house henceforth respected. The Dutchman from Europe can lease native land, but he cannot definitely own it by purchase. He can invest his capital in Dutch East Indian mining or agriculture, and the government will levy taxes, the proceeds of which go to the further development and protection of Dutch East Indian interests, that is to say, to the further education in manifold ways and directions of the native population, nearly eight times as large as that of the lowlands on the North Sea. Every detail of this is organized on the spot by a government service, consisting of less than 12000 European civil servants, assisted by a native personnel of about 450.000. Of the small but effective Dutch East Indian army, 35.000 men in all, the greater part (27.000 men) is also recruited from amongst the natives. Again, the police forces in the Archipelago (totalling about 30.000 men) are almost entirely native, with no more than 1500 Europeans in the higher ranks.

We now obtain a clearer view of facts and proportions. We note that the number of Hollanders living in the East Indies (a little over 200.000, women and children inclusive) is very small indeed, compared to the 60 million natives. In fact, in these Malaysian Islands there is 1 Hollander (man, woman or child) to every 300 natives, and only 1 Hollander exercising a government or private function to every 700 natives. But nevertheless Dutch influence has made itself felt in every corner of these lands, offering safety, order, social and economic betterment, weeding out oriental remnants of brutal barbarism, but respecting scrupulously the constructive principles of native justice, traditions and customs, and restoring with sincere devotion the decaying monuments of the civilizations of the past.

TWO TREES WERE PLANTED IN THE
YEAR 1909, WHEN HOLLAND'S ROYAL
PRINCESS, JULIANA, WAS BORN ~
ONE IN THE COOL SOIL OF HOLLAND'S
NORTHERN CLIMATE. AND ANOTHER
UNDER THE HOT SUN IN THE FERTILE
EARTH OF THE TROPICAL DUTCH EAST
INDIES. EQUAL IN YEARS, CONTRASTING
IN SIZE. TWO SYMBOLS, ONE THOUGHT!

Indeed, the greatest sun-porch of Holland's house is no longer a place in the sun for Dutchmen in search of easy and abundant riches. It has been turned into a large room, one of the largest of the house, where part of the family is organizing its own life with the help and partly with the means and under the protection of the others. It is no lazy spot for sweet slumbers, but has become a workshop by itself, cooperating with the other workrooms of the house in a growing appreciation of a common front.

Of course there have been mistakes, misunderstandings, tactless moments. In a task of such magnitude, mere man is liable to lose his composure in a weaker moment or two. There have also been movements of what one might choose to call native nationalism, impatiently clamouring for immediate and total independence, assiduously and not unselfishly encouraged by foreign communists (who in principle donot recognize any nationalism at all), or by their bitterest enemies, certain foreign pan-Asiatic circles (whose ultimate aim is really and only the strengthening, by means of imperialistic expansion, of *their own* nationalism). But on the whole these influences have not been able to disturb the deeper and more realistic conviction that Holland and the Indies, pooling their fate, can be a constructive team, and that the Dutch as team mates are, from the eastern point of view, preferable to others. They have shown their good intentions, their skill and their means of assistance. They may have their faults, but other people's faults may be much worse. And by educating the native, they at any rate have proved not to be afraid of the intellectual weapon which knowledge places in the native's hand. And so this Dutchman cannot very well be such a bad fellow after all.

We refrain in this story from repeating things about the endless tropical wealth, which everybody knows. Sugar and tea, rubber and coffee, cinchona and tobacco, nutmeg and pepper, palm- and mineral oil, gold and tin, coal and silver, have undoubtedly played their part in the history of the Dutch East Indies. Without them, Holland might never have ventured out into the far east, and never have had to face the tremendous building job which began by profiteering and turned into a most difficult but most inspired contribution to twentieth century human society. The days of the old Dutch East India Company, of an energetic, courageous and skilful but necessarily one-sided commercial spirit of 'giving too little and asking too much' as a critical song would have it, are over. A New Deal is offered to the Indies. Unlike in the olden times the door of Holland's sun-porch remains also wide open to *foreign* enterprise, in so far as foreign business or capital, seeking legitimate profit, can contribute to the development and welfare of the Archipelago. As a matter of fact 65% of the capital invested in new industries between the years 1929 and 1939, was of foreign origin. Holland itself has shown its confidence in India's future by putting approximately 23% of its national wealth into this far eastern work of art. This attitude, coupled with a wise policy of avoiding international entanglements, and of building up an efficient military and naval defense, may produce the best possible guarantees for a peaceful evolution in this part of the world. And *that* is something in which mightier empires than the Netherlands are interested. Or should be.

In the western hemisphere: Holland in the Americas, the

sun-porches are perhaps less spectacular because of their much smaller size and infinitely smaller population. In Dutch Guyana, eastward of Venezuela and British Guyana, the inhabitants, numbering about 170.000, are chiefly negroes, maroons, immigrated Javanese and British Indian natives. Less than 3000 Europeans have settled there. The process of economic and social building is hampered by a comparatively poor soil, and by lack of manual labour and available capital, although in certain mineral lines [bauxite for instance], American participation has achieved excellent results, and certain fruitgrowing propositions are considered to be quite promising.

Spreading over the Caribbean Sea are the Dutch isles of Curaçao, Aruba and Bonaire, near the Venezuela coast, and further north west, the islets of St. Eustatius, Saba and St. Martin. Oil refineries, tank-shipping and fuelling-services have furnished an economic basis for an amazingly rapid increase of inhabitants and opportunity, placing Curaçao in the class of the second seaport of Europe. Still, up to now the total population of the six islands remains below one hundred thousand. The same process of evolution through spiritual, intellectual, political and technical education repeats itself, though not of course, with the dimensions prevailing on the gigantic far eastern scene. Surely, for the Dutch social and political architects, engaged in consolidating the sun-porches of Holland's house, the end of their labors is by no means in sight!

The Dutch nation, experience has shown, seems to be eminently equipped for the performance of a 'colonial' task which requires in its modern conception above all things — according to one of the shrewdest advisors of the government — 'patience allied to doggedness, cautiousness allied to energy, thoroughness allied to a familiar and easy going manner, idealism as well as matter-of-factness, and a critical sense joined with tolerance'. 'Let the Dutch nation — he concluded — therefore, by giving its very best to the task overseas, and by making its national spirit serve the good cause of cooperation between East and West, prove that it is the worthy successor to an honourable past.'

That is precisely what these men behind their dikes, but also versed in scanning far horizons to widen their vision and the scope of their achievements, are doing and will do.

As for napping, not here!

XI. INTERIOR DECORATION

Freedom! As a nation the Dutch conquered it in the 17th century. As a political right of the individual citizen, they received it in 1848 when democratic government was consolidated in the constitutional and parliamentary monarchy, with the ministers of the crown being responsible to the duly elected representatives of the people. As the ultimate gift of this process of political development, they obtained, early in our 20th century, universal suffrage for both sexes over 25 years of age, and proportional representation. Today more than 3½ out of 8 million Dutchmen are entitled to vote, and thereby to exert political influence.

A free people living in a free state. But freedom is no end in itself. It is a principle to be worked out in a social and political system, the aim of which must be the spiritual and material welfare of the community, so that every individual life may use its own forces, responsibility and talents under the best possible circumstances. The organization of these circumstances in Holland's house marks, in this story, the extent of its 'interior decoration'.

Man cannot live by bread alone. But bread is an essential element in his life. 'Poverty'—as someone said—'may be no disgrace, but that is about the only nice thing you can say about it.' In other words, a certain amount of physical and material security is necessary for the great majority of people who must live on what they are able to earn with their heads and hands, without other capital to fall back on, before the other valuable things in life, that is: other than 'bread', can get a decent chance. The recognition of this elementary wisdom was the ouverture of Holland's social New Deal.

Women and children first! It is part of a code that an old seafaring nation was bound to understand after somebody drew their attention to certain dangers connected with modern industrialization. In 1874, more than half a century ago, a law was passed placing restrictions on the use of child labor. It meant an experiment, at first with disappointing results. But it made people think, and the rumble of an oncoming labor movement — very radical in its first appearances — made them think twice. And so in 1889 the scope of the law was extended over women and children, and shortly afterwards the principle was admitted that even full grown men might need legal protection against the turbulent age of machines, mass production and intensive industrial methods. Meanwhile trade unionism began to flourish. Today more than 25% of Dutch labor is organized.

Social legislation had started on its course. Government control gradually reached out further, but at first only to suppress improper, dangerous or abusive practices in mines or factories, by limiting working hours, by forbidding young persons or women to perform certain kinds of labor or night-work, and by ordaining technical safety-measures in workshops. At the same time the government began to take an interest in the housing conditions of the poorer classes by drawing up certain minimum standards and by creating credit-facilities for new building projects. Today on a national total of about $1^3/_4$ million houses the slums count less than $3^1/_2\%$ in number.

Evolution towards a decent job in a decent place, for a decent man in a decent home, and with the government supervising decent conditions, is gradually making its way. And parallel with it grows social insurance, against accidents in the factory, at sea, on the farm, and against the financial consequences of sickness, disablement and old age. A large and complicated structure of social machinery has been put together. And it goes without saying that this development has met with different trends of opinion amongst the parties concerned: labor, the employer, the consumer, the eternal taxpayer and their political parties. For it is clear that this kind of evolution must have next to its desirable social results, widespread financial and economic consequences for a much larger group than the working men directly concerned.

There is also the hotly debated question as to whether the impartial government or the private or organized employer in cooperation with organized labor is better equipped to apply these various forms of social provision in the most efficient, businesslike and economical manner. There is the old controversy as to whether there must be *more* or *less* government in business. There is the fear on the one side, and the wish on the other, that the economic life of the nation will or should be taken in hand as a whole by the government or its agencies, to be directed with 'managed production', 'managed currency', 'managed distribution of capital' or whatever the object to be 'managed' may have to be in particular, 'managed tariff policy' not to be forgotten.

Those who believe that the enormous economic, social as well as moral problem of unemployment can only be solved by the united effort of the entire country with all its reserves of men, material and capital, aspire at the construction of an organic society, in which the government, or trade corporations along the modernized lines of the ancient guilds and under final government supervision, would coordinate the total activities, limiting the individual scope and competitive opportunities of everyone for the general good. Others point to the dangerous inclination of all such systems to stimulate irresponsible slackness, or to encroach upon the individual rights of the independent business man, employer and citizen, no longer free to choose his own course and his own risks. They also fear that ultimately the *economic* dictatorship of the state must lead to a loss of *political* liberty, because there will come a moment when the 'managing' state becomes so heavily involved in what used to be private economic enterprise, and perhaps economic loss, that it will no more permit opposition in this new 'business' than the leader of a private concern would allow any in his without firing his opponents. The difference being that a private individual can leave an employer with whom he disagrees, but no one can leave a state which can force its citizens to stay and obey even to the point of suffocating.

In the house that Holland built, all these opinions and more can be found today in all the rooms, not leaving out the sunporches. It may be taken for granted that all the members of the family have the family-interests truly and constantly in mind, even if they donot agree about the best ways to serve them. But this is by no means a Dutch 'spécialité de la maison'. The same confusion can be observed in most countries, where healthy freedom of opinion and opposition, albeit loyal opposition, still prevail. So we will not go into that any further. It

BRINGING HOME THE BACON IS
NOT SO EASY IN TIMES OF WORLD
CRISIS AND ALL THAT SORT OF THING.
BUT THE THRIFTY HOLLANDERS
HAVE SUCCEEDED IN DEVELOPING
A SPECIAL KIND OF ANIMAL TO
HELP THEM SEE IT THROUGH:

THE STONEWARE SAVING-PIG.

is a matter of method, not of ultimate aim. The international situation has completely disorganized a natural exchange of goods, capital and services between the nations. Under such circumstances every individual nation is forced to apply abnormal remedies. They may—in Holland at least—affect the form, but not the purpose of the interior decoration of the house; this purpose being that each member of the national community must be assisted, *if necessary*, to achieve by his own energy, supplemented by his employer or by the state, a reasonable guarantee for a reasonable basis of existence.

There are more ways than one which can lead up to this. Energy can yield better returns, and not only in a materialistic conception, when sharpened by knowledge, that is to say by education. In Holland's house the schoolroom has always been one of the favorite topics of conversation, disagreement and action. After long and painful political struggles the primary (so called neutral) public school and those based on religious principles in a great many interpretations, have been given equal claims on the national exchequer. And now Holland is busily teaching its young generations with all sorts of educational systems, spreading an enormous network of educational opportunities, from the primary schoolbenches up to the universities and other exalted regions of science, which produced amongst many remarkable men of learning, no fewer than 9 Dutch winners of Nobel prizes, four in physics, two in chemistry, two in physiology and medecine, and one for peace.

Education and a reasonable chance in life to use it, in decent surroundings and under healthy conditions, those are the chief parts of the outfit which Holland's house endeavours to offer to its occupants. But conditions must not be the only healthy matter. The people themselves must be able to raise a healthy mind in a healthy body. A small nation, forced by circumstances to make intensive use of every available opportunity in its struggle for life, must have an open eye for physical culture and fitness. Therefore private initiative as well as the public health services of the government have built up extensive organizations for free·or almost free medical control, preventive treatment, the dissemination of hygienic information, hospital- and sanatorium-service, special facilities for young mothers and babies, etc. And an increasing interest in outdoor sports, in hiking and camping, in the open air work of Boy Scouts, Girl Guides and the like, will in the long run help to reduce the average Dutchman's weight, increase his height, provide him with a streamline model and a fashionable tan on his cheeks. The Olympic Games of 1928 in Amsterdam, and the World Jamboree of 1937 at Vogelenzang, near the famous Dutch bulbfields, have left imperishable souvenirs in scores of athletic hearts. Be fit or get off!, is rapidly becoming the cry of an outspoken younger generation. Although life teaches pretty soon to take a milder view. But having started in high, they can afford to slow down a mile per hour or so. Meanwhile the birthrate in Holland is about 20 per thousand, and the death rate 8,8, the lowest in all the world, as we said before. That tells a story by itself.

For the last ten years the economic and political world confusion has cast a shadow over this 'Dutch interior' which must now take care of between 3 and 400.000 unemployed. But in stormy weather the Hollanders have always been able to muster up much more team-spirit than under a blue sky. They are seriously putting their heads together to tackle the obstacle. And it is not at all surprising that plans for creating new work should now come forth, such as have made their appearance on various occasions in Holland's history: Increase the soil! This time not so much by reclaiming more land from the water, but by turning waste land into arable fields on a very large scale. The secret of how to multiply your living-space within your own walls.

The spirit of the house is the spirit of the highly scientific, highly efficient, but also highly emotional and highly temperamental twentieth century, tempered by the cool, calm and collected Dutch mind, a trifle suspicious towards new ideas, and uncommonly matter-of-fact. Social idealism in Holland is being tried out in a businesslike way. It may not produce a flaming elan, but it does take care of the neediest cases, and is carefully willing to do big things. All this without much waving of flags or blaring of trumpets. Perhaps they are wrong there. It pays to advertise.

XII. WELCOME STRANGER!

Tomorrow's world, tomorrow's house . . .

Patiently, and sometimes impatiently, the Dutch have been building at it. The national walls went up during the long war with Spain. The roof was put on when, in 1648, victory came and the sovereign Netherlands were recognized by a surprised world. Enlargements followed when Dutch ships brought settlers to the far east and the Americas. The rules of the house were drawn up in a spirit of tolerance and freedom, and of unswerving loyalty to that pioneering dynasty, founded by William the Silent, who dared to lead the way when the future looked hopeless.

The house was furnished with goods and institutions into which Dutch sweat and blood had gone. It was decorated with the cultural achievements of a nation, feverishly studying, under a phlegmatic outward appearance, the science, the literature, the philosophies, the music, the paintings of an outside world so very much larger than the house itself, and generously giving to that world, in exchange, its own contributions to human culture. The garden, intensively cultivated, yielded excellent things of which a normal world was in constant need. The fishpond and the boathouse were scenes of the keenest activity. The industrial workshop was humming. The equatorial sun-porches were turned into well equipped living quarters. The schoolrooms were full of eager younger generations. The pantry was comfortably stocked. And in the safe something had been carefully stored away for a rainy day: the fruit of hard work and conservative finance.

Welcome stranger! Come and rest a while in Holland's house, a small corner of a large earth, but seasoned through the ages with the experience of a self-made nation. 'God has created the world, with the exception of Holland—*that* was created by the Dutch themselves', a light-spirited Frenchman once said. And in some respects this is true. Soil recovered from water, independence wrestled from foreign tyranny, both paid for with human life and human blood. Unity achieved under the threat of common danger. Religious freedom the fruit of religious war. Political freedom the heritage of that philosophy of tolerance which had to be defended at the point of swords and guns against the Spanish Inquisition. Considering all this, it is not so surprising that the Dutch should have become a comparatively distrusting nation, jealously guarding the material and spiritual values which they gained at such great pains, and very carefully investigating every fresh and perhaps alluring idea, adventure or principle that presents itself, before exposing the house and all it stands for to new risks. Careful, yes, but investigating all the same. For Holland's house must remain up to date, lest it should become something to be placed behind glass in the world's archaeological museums.

Go and see it fully alive! Welcome stranger, once again! If it's true that architecture is the printing press of all ages and expresses the spirit of the place and time in which it was conceived, the modern houses, public buildings and residential suburbs of Holland's old, historical cities will tell an amazing story of restless probing into the possibilities of logical and harmonious synthesis of true form and modern material. Certainly, the traditional tulip, the full trousers, the wooden shoes,

WELCOME STRANGER!

can still be seen, but from a network of brandnew roads for motor traffic, or from the air or from trains with the latest in electric or Diesel-traction. There are still old fashioned sails to be found gliding along the canals, the lakes and the big herring pond, weaving patches of white and grey and reddish brown into the colour schemes of nature. But there are also high-powered speedboats, and floating castles of international reputation, equipped with all the comfort and luxuries which the Vikings of this age require for an errand of less than a week on the ocean. There are 15th century primitives to be admired in Holland's museums, and the exuberant masters of the age of Rembrandt, Hals, Steen and Ruysdael. But there are also vigorous interpreters of a new age of reason and even unreason, coming after the expressionism of Vincent van Gogh. There is a thirst for the music of all times and the next, which has made it possible to create, in this small but busy country, some of the finest symphony orchestras of the world under the leadership of Willem Mengelberg, whose name needs no introduction, and others. There is, for those who can master the tongue a classical literature of great beauty, wisdom and erudition, but also the burning faith or the nervously penetrating analytical mind of a present day generation, longing for something wider than a world full of barriers, bursting with neo-romantic passion for an inner life without compromise.

Yes, Holland's house is very much alive, and the people in it spend their time by no means in easy chairs or warming their feet at the fireside. They know that the work of building tomorrow's world never ends, and they keep on building, hitting high marks sometimes, making occasional errors of taste or judgement, stumbling over some of their problems, but always getting up again to try anew. People, with their roots reaching deeply into their comparatively narrow strip of land. For equatorial Holland, east and west, may need Dutch technical, educational, scientific, economic and political leadership, it can never, on account of its tropical conditions and native interests, become a field for mass-immigration from the Netherlands. The Hollander knows this. He must make the most of his own European corner, watch the world and cooperate with it, wherever possible, and invite the world in turn to come and watch him at work. He teaches his children many foreign languages, he travels much and far as soon as he can afford it, he reads foreign books and newspapers, he listens on the radio to speakers from the far corners of the earth. His air-liners travel in regular services across three continents from Amsterdam to Batavia and Sydney and back. And pretty soon they may establish direct trans-oceanic links with the West Indies, where a Dutch local air-way-system already operates. His steamers cover the seven seas, and the largest of them all plies between Rotterdam and New York, bearing the old name of 'New Amsterdam' as an inspiring echo from the past.

In this spirit the Hollander feels at ease in the world. And in this same spirit of comradeship he likes to show his house to others. How it *was* built, how it *is* being renovated, how worth while old furniture is honored and kept, without forgetting that time goes on, how green the meadows are, how fragrant the flowerbeds, how nice it smells in the kitchen, if one knows where to find the right kitchen for all the specialities of the menu. And butter and cheese, Zeeland oysters, Holland gin, cigars and a real Dutch beefsteak are by no means the only stars on this culinary firmament.

Only, inside advice is to be recommended. Ask the Dutch Tourist Office. They know. But do not believe the otherwise amiable Erasmus when he writes that the Dutch are 'a hungry run of people, born exclusively for their tummies'. That was not even true of his 16th century contemporaries. They may have loved their food and wine, but they also fought for freedom and founded a far eastern stronghold and New Netherland in America. Which is the sort of open air adventure overfed people usually dislike for obvious reasons.

We have reached the end of our story. And because it is addressed in the first place to that new world of tomorrow which is shaping its destinies in the United States, we feel justified in recalling a charming historical scene: the record of one fine day in 1776, when both the houses of Holland and of America were fairly or extremely young. The American war of independence was still undecided, when a vessel, flying the colours of the revolutionists, passed the little Dutch isle of St. Eustatius, east of Portorico. The governor, perhaps remembering the revolutionary birth of his own country, two hundred years earlier, officially saluted this new symbol, a fresh contribution to a free world, and hoisted the red, white and blue. But an English fleet got wind of this, and punished the Dutchman's gesture by confiscating on the island a large quantity of merchandise and a number of ships. However, by doing this the British admiral—so the story goes—lost so much time that he arrived too late in the indomitable North American

JOHANNES VAN DER STEEN
OF AMSTERDAM, ANNO 1626
THE COMMON ANCESTOR OF

MIJNHEER JAN
VAN DER STEEN
OF PRESENT-DAY
THE HAGUE....

....AND MR. JOHN
VANDERSTONE
OF ALBANY 1939

colonies to turn the scales in England's favor. Must we conclude that a gallant Dutch governor in the West Indies unwittingly decided America's fate? If this should seem too good to be true, it must be set down in this narrative nevertheless. For it *ought* to have happened anyway.

Dutch resistance breaking the power of Spain three centuries ago, started a new ideal of political liberty. Through this political manifestation of the spirit of the Renaissance the right of national self determination victoriously asserted itself. America was to follow in its own time.

But rights must be used, and wisely so. It is the building up of something, on the basis of just and decent conceptions, that counts. And Holland has earnestly been trying to do just that. We are inclined to agree with dr. Hendrik Willem van Loon, Holland-American historian and great admirer of Erasmus, when in his essay on 'Multiplex Man' he offers a thought that might well become the device on the banners of all those who are doing their bit to prepare tomorrow's world by improving the one of today.

'Above all things—our sage proclaims—man shall say 'yes' to Life, and armed with patience and forbearance and good, natured humour, he shall relentlessly push forward into the realm of the unknown, until the little drop of energy which he has borrowed for a short space of time shall be needed for some other purpose, when he expects to surrender the loan without a single word of regret, as he has learned that both life and death are but expressions of one and the same idea, and that nothing really counts in this world except the courage with which the individual has dared to attack the one problem of which there is no definite solution: the problem of existence'.

The problem remains. After tomorrow's world there will be another one.

And in the house of Holland work continues, along the whole line.

Marching on.

New Amsterdam, April 1939.

PRINTED ON PAPER SUPPLIED BY

G. H. Bührmann Paper Company Inc.

Amsterdam

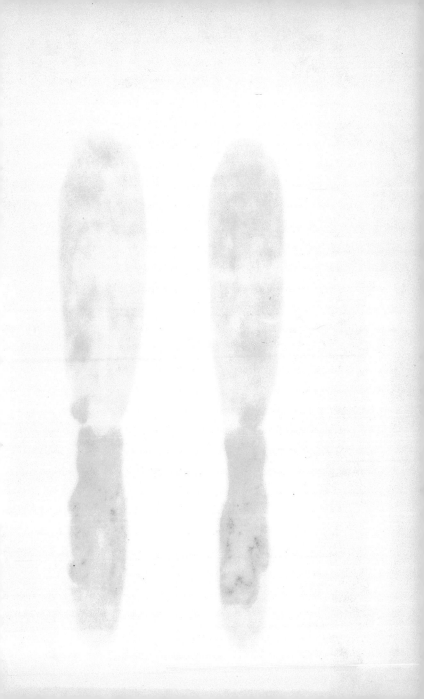

24095

DJ
109
B7

BRICKLAYER, PETER
    HOLLAND'S HOUSE.

DATE DUE

GAYLORD   PRINTED IN U.S.A.